Native American Legends:

Stories of the
Hopi Indians
Vol. One

Written and Edited by
G.W. Mullins
With Original Art by
C.L. Hause

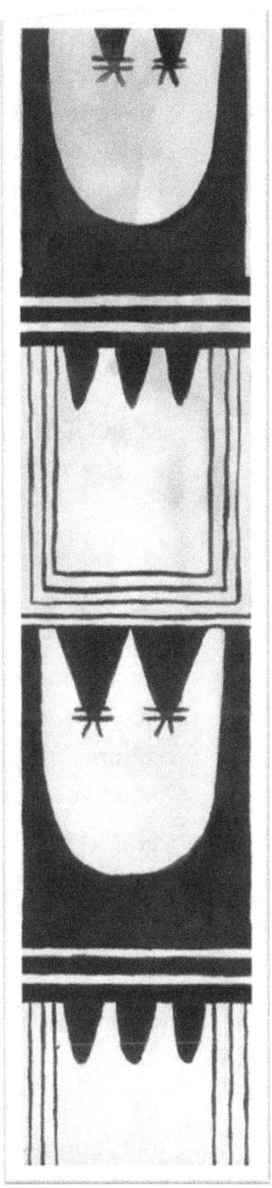

ISBN: 978-1-7377100-2-8

Second Edition Printing

Light Of The Moon Publishing has allowed this work to remain exactly as the author intended, verbatim, without editorial input.

Printed in the United States of America

The following book represents a collection of Native American works which are public domain. You may have read the stories before. In true story telling fashion, the stories have been left as close to the original form as possible. In Native American culture, in order to pass the stories along with all information intact, they had to be told pretty much word for word, to keep the legends alive. Many of these stories were translated directly from original Native language texts. With that in mind, please be aware that some spellings and word usage may vary from one tribe to another. For instance, the spelling of "teepee", as used in this book, can also be written as "tipi", and "tepee". All are correct. Also, when using words like "someone", in most native cultures, it would be "some one". So, keep in mind, these are not necessarily misspellings. They are simply dialect and translations.

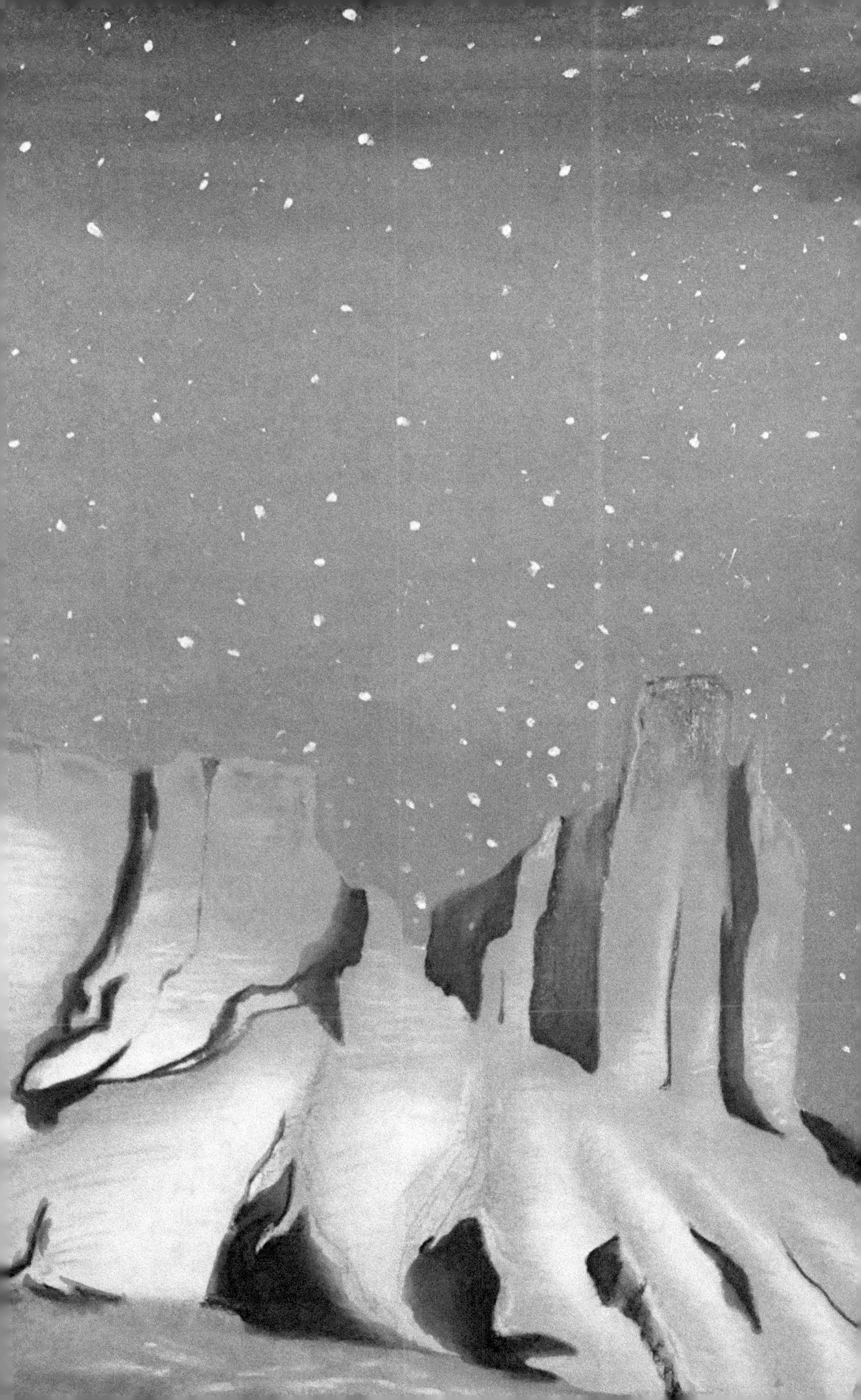

This book is dedicated to Vince Mullins, my Grandfather (Pawpaw). He was a tall red man with fire in his eyes… who I loved so much.

G.W. Mullins

This book is also dedicated to Chief Dan George, a true visionary.

"May the stars carry your sadness away,
May the flowers fill your heart with beauty,
May hope forever wipe away your tears,
And, above all, may silence make you strong."

~ Chief Dan George

Chief Dan George, (July 24, 1899 – September 23, 1981) was a chief of the Tsleil-Waututh Nation, a Coast Salish band located on Burrard Inlet in North Vancouver, British Columbia, Canada. He was also an author, poet, actor, and an Officer of the Order of Canada. At the age of 71, he was nominated for an Academy Award for Best Supporting Actor in Little Big Man.

Also Available From G.W. Mullins And C.L. Hause

More Star People, Sky Gods And Other Paranormal Tales Of The Native American Indians

Walking With Spirits Native American Myths, Legends, And Folklore Volumes One Thru Six

The Native American Cookbook

Native American Cooking - An Indian Cookbook With Legends And Folklore

The Native American Story Book - Stories Of The American Indians For Children Volumes One Thru Five

The Best Native American Stories For Children

Cherokee A Collection of American Indian Legends, Stories And Fables

Creation Myths - Tales Of The Native American Indians

Strange Tales Of The Native American Indians

Spirit Quest - Stories Of The Native American Indians

Animal Tales Of The Native American Indians

Medicine Man - Shamanism, Natural Healing, Remedies And Stories Of The Native American Indians

Native American Legends: Stories Of The Hopi Indians Volumes One and Two

Totem Animals Of The Native Americans

The Best Native American Myths, Legends And Folklore Volumes One Thru Three

Ghosts, Spirits And The Afterlife In Native American Indian Mythology And Folklore

The Native American Art Book – Art Inspired By Native American Myths And Legends

Star People, Sky Gods And Other Tales Of The Native American Indians

THE NATIVE AMERICAN STORY COLLECTION SERIES

Featuring The Writing Of Best-Selling Author

G.W. MULLINS

And Original Art From Award Winning Artist C.L. HAUSE

The Native American Story Book Series / The Best Native American Stories For Children

Tales Of The Native American Indians / Native American Legends Series

Native American Cooking, Art And Medicine Books

Walking With Spirits Native American Myths, Legends, And Folklore Series

The Best Native American Myths, Legends And Folklore / Supernatural Tales

Walking With Spirits Volumes 1 thru 6
Native American Myths, Legends, And Folklore

The Native American Cookbook

The Best Native American Stories for Children

Native American Cooking -
An Indian Cookbook With Legends And Folklore

The Native American Story Book Volumes 1 thru 5
Stories Of The American Indians For Children

Creation Myths - Tales Of The Native American Indians

Strange Tales Of The Native American Indians

Animal Tales Of The Native American Indians

Spirit Quest Native American Indian Legends Stories and Fables

Medicine Man - Shamanism, Natural Healing, Remedies And Stories Of The Native American Indians

Cherokee A Collection of American Indian Legends, Stories And Fables

Native American Legends: Stories Of The Hopi Indians Volumes One and Two

The Native American Art Book

The Best Native American Myths, Legends And Folklore Vols 1-3

Ghosts, Spirits And The Afterlife In Native American Indian Mythology And Folklore

Supernatural Tales Of The Native American Indians

The Song of Creation - A Hopi Legend

The dark purple light rises in the north,
A yellow light rises in the east.
Then we of the flowers of the earth come forth
To receive a long life full of joy.
We call ourselves the Butterfly maidens.

Both male and female make their prayers to the east,
Make the respectful sign to the Sun, our Creator.
The sounds of bells ring through the air,
Making a joyful sound throughout the land,
Their joyful echo resounding everywhere.

Humbly I ask my Father,
The perfect one, Taiowa, our Father,
The perfect one, creating the beautiful life
Shown to us by the yellow light,
To give us perfect light at the time of the red light.

The perfect one laid out the perfect plan
And gave to us a long span of life,
Creating song to implant joy in life.
On this path of happiness, we the Butterfly maidens
Carry out his wishes by greeting our Father Sun.

The song resounds back from our Creator with joy,
And we of the earth repeat it to our Creator.
At the appearing of the yellow light,
Repeats and repeats again in the joyful echo,
Sounds and resounds for times to come.

The First People of the First World did not answer her: they could not speak. Something had to be done. Since Spider Woman received her power from Sótuknang, she had to call him and ask him what to do. So she called

Palöngawhoya and said, "Call your Uncle. We need him at once."

Palöngawhoya, the echo twin, sent out his call along the world axis to the vibratory centers of the earth, which resounded his message throughout the universe. "Sótuknang, our Uncle, come at once! We need you!" All at once, with the sound of a mighty wind, Sótuknang appeared in front of them. "I am here, why do you need me so urgently?"

Spider Woman explained, "As you commanded me, I have created these First People. They are fully and firmly formed, they are properly colored, they have life and movement. But they cannot talk. That is the proper thing they lack. So I want you to give them speech. Also the wisdom and the power to reproduce, so that they might enjoy their life and give thanks to the Creator."

So Sótuknang gave them speech, a different language to each color, with respect for each other's difference. He also gave them the wisdom and the power to reproduce and multiply.

Then he said to them, "With all these I have given you this world to live on and to be happy. There is only one thing I ask of you: to respect the Creator at all times. Wisdom, harmony, and respect for the love of the Creator who made you: may it grow and never be forgotten among you as long as you live."

So, the First People went their directions, were happy, and began to multiply.

Hopi Prayer For Peace

"Great Spirit and all unseen, this day we pray and ask You for guidance, humbly we ask You to help us and fellow men to have recourse to peaceful ways of life, because of uncontrolled deceitfulness by human- kind. Help us all to love, not hate one another.

We ask you to be seen in an image of Love and Peace. Let us be seen in beauty, the colors of the rainbow. We respect our Mother, the planet, with our loving care, for from Her breast we receive our nourishment.

Let us not listen to the voices of the two-hearted, the destroyers of mind, the haters and self-made leaders, whose lusts for power and wealth will lead us into confusion and darkness.

Seek visions always of world beauty, not violence nor battlefields.

It is our duty to pray always for harmony between man and earth, so that the earth will bloom once more. Let us show our emblem of love and goodwill for all life and land.

Pray for the House of Glass, for within it are minds clear and pure as ice and mountain streams. Pray for the great leaders of nations in the House of Mica who in their own quiet ways help the earth in balance.

We pray the Great Spirit that one day our Mother Earth will be purified into a healthy peaceful one. Let us sing for strength of wisdom with all nations for the good of all people. Our hope is not yet lost, purification must be to restore the health of our Mother Earth for lasting peace and happiness.

Techqua Ikachi – for Land and Life!"

Contents

Introduction

Native American Indian culture is known for its rich oral traditions. In many cases there were no written languages to document their histories. The tribes relied on verbal communication to share their customs, history, rituals and legends.

The tribal elders used vibrant tales to pass information to the younger generations. These stories were not only related to tribal history but were meant to entertain as well as educate, while preserving their tribal culture.

Each time an elder told a story, new life was breathed into it. The telling of the stories gave a revived meaning to the tribe's past and their relations to the earth and the animals they had depended on for existence. In many cases when the stories were told, they were accompanied by music. Drums and rhythm were paired with dance to create a visual record.

The Hopi Indians culture was and is rich with these stories. With a past stretching back thousands of years, they are one of the oldest living cultures in documented history. The tribe's teachings relate stories of a great flood and other events dating to ancient times. The Hopi trace their ancestry back to the Ancient Puebloan and Basketmaker cultures. They were responsible for many stone structures and artifacts of the Grand Canyon and across the Southwest. A deeply religious people, they live by the ethic of peace and goodwill.

There was a time in Hopi history that when crops were harvested, religious ceremonies had been performed, and the winter wood had been collected. It was at this time that the people broke out into dance and story-telling. It was a time of sharing a rich history. With this book, that time is now.

Included in this book, which is one of two volumes is a huge collection of the stories of the Hopi Indians. Without books and without writing the Hopi have an extensive literature. These stories have been collected with the main purpose of preserving the ancient stories of Native American life. Over the years, many collectors have recorded several versions of some of these tales. So keep in mind there is some variation to what has been collected. You are invited to enjoy the culture and as in true Native tradition, share these stories with the next generation.

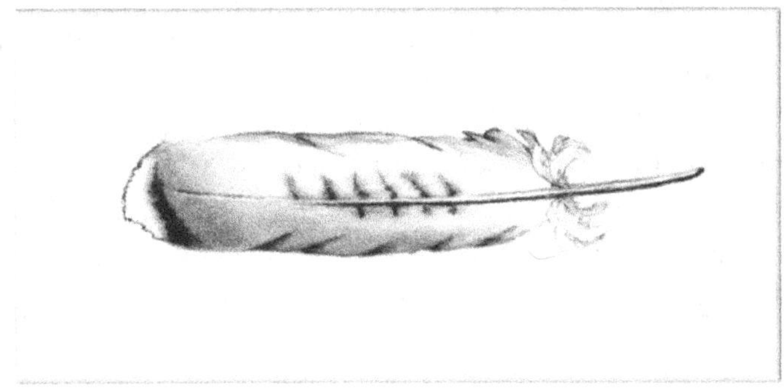

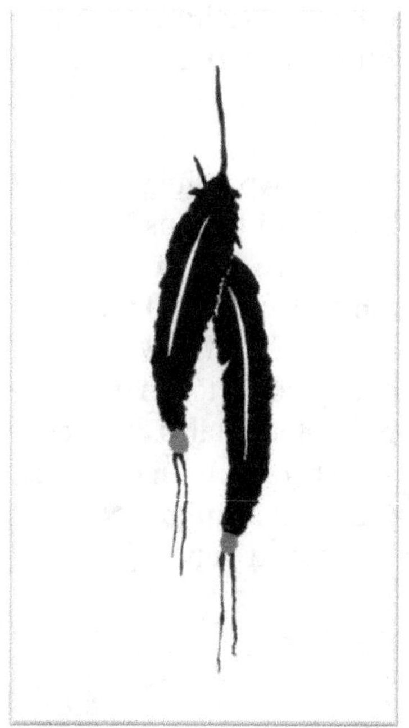

The White Dawn of Hopi

Hopi

A very long time ago, there was nothing but water on the earth. In the east a Huruing Wuhti, one of the goddesses of rocks, clay, minerals, and other hard substances, lived in the ocean. Her house was a kiva, like the kivas of the Hopi today. Two fox skins, one gray, one yellow, were usually tied to the ladder leading into the house. In the west lived another Huruing Wuhti in a similar kiva, with a turtle-shell rattle attached to her ladder.

The sun rose and set on this world of water. Shortly before he appeared in the east, he dressed himself in the skin of the gray fox, creating the white dawn of the Hopi. After a little while he took off the gray skin and put on the yellow skin, which brightened the sky into the yellow dawn of the Hopi. Then he rose, emerging from the opening in the north end of the kiva in which the Huruing Wuhti lived. When he had crossed the sky and arrived in the west, he announced his arrival at the western Huruing Wuhti's kiva by fastening the rattle on the top of the ladder beam. Then he entered the kiva, passed through an opening in its north end, and continued his course eastward under the water.

By and by, the two goddesses caused the waters to recede eastward and westward so that some dry land appeared. The sun passing over the land noticed that no living being could be seen. When he mentioned this to the goddesses, the one in the west invited the one in the east to come and talk about it. The Huruing Wuhti of the east traveled west over a rainbow, and the two deities deliberated and decided to create a little bird.

The Huruing Wuhti of the east made a wren of day and covered it up with a piece of *mochapu,* native cloth. Both goddesses sang a song over it, and after a while a live bird came forth. Since the sun always passed over the middle of the earth, the deities thought that he might not have seen living creatures in the north or the south. They sent the little wren to fly all over the earth, but it returned and said that no living being existed anywhere. (Actually Spider Woman, lived in a kiva somewhere in the southwest at the edge of the water, but the little bird failed to notice her.)

The deity of the west proceeded to make many birds of different kinds, covering them with the same cloth under which the wren had been brought to life. Both Huruing Wuhtis again sang a song over them, and presently the birds began to move under the cover. The goddesses took them out, taught every bird the sound that it should make, and let them scatter in all directions.

Next the Huruing Wuhti of the west made different kinds of animals in the same way, teaching them their own sounds or languages and sending them forth to inhabit the earth. Now the goddesses decided that they would create human beings. The Huruing Wuhti of the east fashioned first a white woman and then a white man out of clay and brought them to life. She made two tablets of a hard substance (tradition does not tell whether it was stone or clay), drew characters on them with a wooden stick, and handed them to the man and woman. The humans did not know what the tablets said, so the deity rubbed the palms of her hands first against the palms of the woman and then against the palms of the man. Suddenly the couple understood the meaning of the tablets. Then the deities taught them their language, after which the goddess of the east took them out of the kiva and led them over a rainbow to her home in the east. They stayed four days, and Huruing Wuhti told them to go and select a place to live. They traveled around a while and, finding a good field, built a small, simple house, similar to those of the Hopi.

Soon the Huruing Wuhti of the west told the eastern goddess, "All this is not finished yet." By then Spider Woman had heard what they were doing, and she also created a man and woman of clay. But she taught them Spanish and fashioned two burros for them, and the couple settled down near her.

Spider Woman continued to create people in the same manner, giving a different language to each pair. But she forgot to make a woman for a certain man, and this is the reason why today there are always some single men. Then as she continued turning out people, she found that she had failed to create a man for a certain woman. "Oh my!" she said, and told the woman, "Somewhere there is a single man who went away. Find him and if he accepts you, live with him. If he doesn't, both of you will have to stay single. Do the best you can."

The two finally found each other, and the woman said, "Where shall we live?" The man answered, "Why, anywhere." He went to work and built a house for them, but before long they began to quarrel.

"I want to live alone," the woman said. "I can cook for myself."

"Yes, but who will get the wood for you and work the fields?" the man said. "We had better stay together." They made up, but it didn't last. They quarreled, separated, came together again, separated again. If they had managed to get along, all the Hopi would live in peace today. But other couples learned quarreling from them; this is why there are so many arguments between husbands and wives.

These were the kind of people that Spider Woman created - rough mannered. The Huruing Wuhti of the west heard about it and soon called the goddess of the east to come over. "I don't want to live here alone," the deity of the west said. "I want some good people around me." So she created a number of people, always in pairs. But wherever Spider Woman's people came into contact with them, there was trouble. Human beings at that time led a nomadic life, feeding mostly on game. Whenever they found rabbits or antelope or deer, they would kill and eat. This led to many quarrels.

Finally the goddess of the west said to the people: "You stay· here; I'm going to live in the middle of the ocean in the west. When you want anything, pray to me there." Her people were sorrowful, but she left them. The Huruing Wuhti of the east did the same, and that's the reason why their kivas are never seen today. Hopi who want something from them must deposit their prayer offerings in the village. And when they say their prayers, they think of the two goddesses who live far away, but who, the Hopi believe, still remember them.

-Based on a story reported in 1905 *by H. R. Voth .*

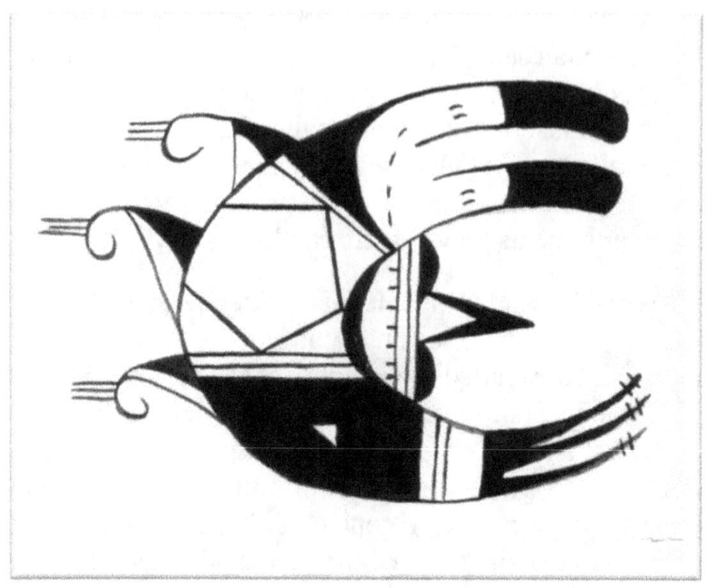

The Pookonghoyas and the Cannibal Monster

A Hopi Legend

H. R. Voth, The Traditions of the Hopi, Field Columbian Museum Anthropological Series, 1905

A very long time ago a large monster, whom our forefathers called Shíta, lived somewhere in the west, and used to come to the village of Oraíbi and wherever it would find children it would devour them.

Often also grown people were eaten by the monster. The people became very much alarmed over the matter, and especially the village chief was very much worried over it. Finally he concluded to ask the Pöokónghoyas for assistance. These latter, namely Pöokónghoya and his younger brother Balö'ngahoya, lived north of and close to the village of Oraíbi. When the village chief asked them to rid them of this monster they told him to make an arrow for each one of them. He did so, using for the shaft feathers, the wing feathers of the bluebird. These arrows he brought to the little War Gods mentioned.

They said to each other: "Now let us go and see whether such a monster exists and whether we can find it." So they first went to Oraíbi and kept on the watch around the village.

One time, when they were on the east side of the village at the edge of the mesa, they noticed something approaching from the west side. They at once went there and saw that it was the monster that they were to destroy. When the monster met the two brothers it said to them: "I eat you" (Shíta). Both brothers objected.

The monster at once swallowed the older one and then the other one. They found that it was not dark inside of the monster, in fact, they found themselves on a path which the younger brother, who had been swallowed last, followed, soon overtaking his older brother.

The two brothers laughed and said to each other: "So this is the way we find it here. We are not going to die here."

They found that the path on which they were going was the esophagus of the monster, which led into its stomach. In the latter they found a great many people of different nationalities which the monster had devoured in different parts of the earth; in fact, they found the stomach to be a little world in itself, with grass, trees, rock, etc.

Before the two brothers had left their home on their expedition to kill the monster, if possible, their grandmother had told them that in case the monster should swallow them too, to try to find its heart; if they could shoot into the heart the monster would die. So they concluded that they would now go in search of the heart of the monster.

They finally found the path which led out of the stomach, and after following that path quite a distance they saw way above them hanging something which they at once concluded must be the heart of the monster. Pöokónghoya at once shot an arrow at it, but failed to reach it, the arrow dropping back. Hereupon his younger brother tried it and his arrow pierced the heart, whereupon the older brother also shot his arrow into the heart. Then it became dark and, the people noticed that the monster was dying.

The Two War Gods and the Two Maidens

A Hopi Legend

H. R. Voth, The Traditions of the Hopi, Field Columbian Museum Anthropological Series, 1905

A long time ago Pöokónghoya and his little brother Balö'ngahoya lived north of the village at the shrine of the Achámali. One day they heard that two beautiful maidens were watching some fields west of the village of Hû'ckovi, of which the ruins may still be seen a few miles north-west of Oraíbi. They concluded that they would go hunting and at the same time visit those two maidens.

When they arrived there the maidens joyfully greeted them and they were joking and teasing each other. The maidens believed that the two brothers had come with the intention to marry them, and they said, in a half-jesting manner, to their suitors: "We will cut off an arm from each one of you, and if you do not die you may own us."

The younger brother was at once willing, saying to his elder brother: "They are beautiful; let us not be afraid of having our arm cut off." The elder brother hesitated, saying, that that would hurt. So the younger brother said, "I am willing," laid his right arm over the edge of the mealing trough at which the maidens had been working, and one of the maidens struck the arm with the upper mealing stone and cut it off, the arm dropping into the trough or bin. His elder brother hereupon laid his arm over the edge of the bin, which consisted of a thin, sharp slab, and the other maiden also cut his arm off with her mealing stone. Now the two brothers said: "If we recover, we shall come after you. Hand us our arm, now." The maidens did so and the two brothers left, each one carrying his severed arm. Arriving at their home north of Oraíbi, they told their grandmother what had happened.

"There," she said, "You have been in something again and have done some mischief."

"Yes," they said, "We met two beautiful maidens and liked them very much, and so we allowed them to cut off our arms. " Very well, she said, "I am going to set you right again." So she asked them to lay down north of the fireplace.

She placed the two arms by their sides, covered them up, whereupon she commenced to sing a song. When she was through singing, she told them now to get up. They did so and found their arms healed. The next day they proceeded to the house of the maidens, who were surprised to see them fully recovered. The older of the two sisters was the prettier one and Pöokónghoya wanted to choose that one. His younger brother protested, saying: "Yesterday you were not willing to have your arm cut off, as you were then afraid, and now you want to have the first choice. I had my arm cut off first and I am going to choose first," to which his elder brother finally consented. They slept with the maidens that night and then left them and returned to their home north of Oraíbi.

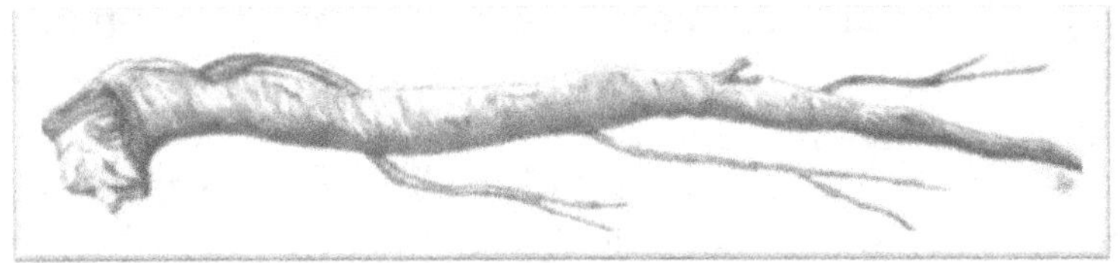

Dug-From Ground

A Hupa Legend

Goddard, University of Cal. Publications in American Archaeology & Ethnology, i, 146, No. 2

An old woman was living with her granddaughter, a virgin. The girl used to go to dig roots and her grandmother used to say to her, "You must not dig those with two stocks." The girl wondered why she was always told that.

One morning she thought, "I am going to dig one," so she went across the river and began digging. She thought, "I am going to take out one with a double stock." When she had dug it out she heard a baby cry. She ran back to the river, and when she got there she heard someone crying "mother" after her.

She jumped into the boat and pushed it across. When she got across, the baby had tumbled down to the other shore. She ran up to the house and there she heard it crying on that side. She ran into the house, then she heard it crying back of the house.

At once she sat down and then she heard it tumble on the roof of the house. The baby tumbled through the smoke-hole and then rolled about on the floor. The old woman jumped up and put it in a baby basket. The young woman sat with her back to the fire and never looked at the child.

The old woman took care of the baby alone. After a time it commenced to sit up and finally to walk. When he was big enough to shoot, the old woman made a bow and he began to kill birds. Afterward he killed all kinds of game; and, because his mother never looked at him, he gave whatever he killed to his grandmother.

Finally he became a man. The young woman had been in the habit of going out at dawn and not returning until dark. She brought back with her acorns as long as her finger. One time the young man thought "I am going to watch and see where she goes."

The young woman had always said to herself, "If he will bring acorns from the place I bring them, and if he will kill a white deer, I will call him my son."

Early one morning the son saw his mother come out of the house and start up the ridge. He followed her and saw her go along until she came to a dry tree. She climbed this and it grew with her to the sky. The young man then returned saying, "Tomorrow I am going up there." The woman came home at night with the usual load of long acorns.

The next morning the man went the way his mother had gone, climbed the tree as he had seen her do, and it grew with him to the sky. When he arrived there he saw a road. He followed that until he came to an oak, which he climbed, and waited to see what would happen. Soon he heard laughing girls approaching.

They came to the tree and began to pick acorns from allotted spaces under it.

The young man began to throw down acorns. "That's right, Bluejay," said one of the girls. Then another said, "It might be Dug-from-the-ground. You can hardly look at him, they say, he is so handsome."

Origin Myth

Told by Qoyawaima (Oraibi)

A very long time ago there was nothing but water. In the east Huruing Wuhti, the deity of all hard substances, lived in the ocean. Her house was a kiva like the kivas of the Hopi of to-day. To the ladder leading into the kiva were usually tied a skin of a gray fox and one of a yellow fox. Another Huruing Wuhti lived in the ocean in the west in a similar kiva, but to her ladder was attached a turtle-shell rattle.

The Sun also existed at that time. Shortly before rising in the east the Sun would dress up in the skin of the gray fox, whereupon it would begin to dawn--the so-called white dawn of the Hopi. After a little while the Sun would lay off the gray skin and put on the yellow fox skin, whereupon the bright dawn of the morning--the so-called yellow dawn of the Hopi--would appear. The Sun would then rise, that is, emerge from an opening in the north end of the kiva in which Huruing Wuhti lived. When arriving in the west again, the sun would first announce his arrival by fastening the rattle on the point of the ladder beam, whereupon he would enter the kiva, pass through an opening in the north end of the kiva, and continue his course eastward under the water and so on.

By and by these two deities caused some dry land to appear in the midst of the water, the waters receding eastward and westward. The Sun passing over this dry land constantly took notice of the fact, that no living being of any kind could be seen anywhere, and mentioned this fact to the two deities. So one time the Huruing Wuhti of the west sent word through the Sun to the Huruing Wuhti in the east to come over to her as she wanted to talk over this matter. The Huruing Wuhti of the east complied with this request and proceeded to the West over a rainbow. After consulting each other on this point the two concluded that they would create a little bird; so the deity of the east made a wren of clay, and covered it up with a piece of native cloth (mochapu). Hereupon they sang a song over it, and after a little while the little bird showed signs of life. Uncovering it, a live bird came forth, saying: "Uma hinok pas nui kita' nawakna?" (Why do you want me so quickly). "Yes," they said, "we want you to fly all over this dry place and see whether you can find anything living." They thought that as the Sun always passed over the middle of the earth, he might have failed to notice any living beings that might exist in the north or the south. So the little Wren, flew all over the earth, but upon its return reported that no living being existed anywhere. Tradition says, however, that by this time Spider Woman (Kohk'ang Wuhti), lived somewhere in the south-west at the edge of the water, also in a kiva, but this the little bird had failed to notice.

Hereupon the deity of the west proceeded to make very many birds of different kinds and form, placing them again under the same cover under which the Wren had been brought, to life. They again sang a song over them. Presently the birds began to move under the cover. The goddess removed the cover and found under it all kinds of birds and fowls. "Why do you want us so quickly?" the latter asked. "Yes, we want you to inhabit this world."

Hereupon the two deities taught every kind of bird the sound that it should make, and then the birds scattered out in all directions.

Hereupon the Huruing Wuhti of the west made of clay all different kinds of animals, and they were brought to life in the same manner as the birds. They also asked the same question: "Why do you want us so quickly?" "We want you to inhabit this earth," was the reply given them, whereupon they were taught by their creators their different sounds or languages, after which they proceeded forth to inhabit the different parts of the earth. They now concluded that they would create man. The deity of the east made of clay first a woman and then a man, who were brought to life in exactly the same manner as the birds and animals before them. They asked the same question, and were told that they should live upon this earth and should understand everything. Hereupon the Huruing Wuhti of the east made two tablets of some hard substance, whether stone or clay tradition does not say, and drew upon them with the wooden stick certain characters, handing these tablets to the newly created man and woman, who looked at them, but did not know what they meant. So the deity of the east rubbed with the palms of her hands, first the palms of the woman and then the palms of the man, by which they were enlightened so that they understood the writing on the tablets. Hereupon the deities taught these two a language.

After they had taught them the language, the goddess of the east took them out of the kiva and led them over a rainbow, to her home in the east. There they stayed four days, after which Huruing Wuhti told them to go now and select for themselves a place and live there. The two proceeded forth saying that they would travel around a while and wherever they would find a good field they would remain. Finding a nice place at last, they built a small, simple house, similar to the old houses of the Hopi. Soon the Huruing Wuhti of the west began to think of the matter again, and said to herself: "This is not the way yet that it should be. We are not done yet," and communicated her thoughts to the Huruing Wuhti of the east. By this time Spider Woman had heard about all this matter and she concluded to anticipate the others and also create some beings. So she also made a man and woman of clay, covered them up, sang over them, and brought to life her handiwork. But these two proved to be Spaniards. She taught them the Spanish language, also giving them similar tablets and imparting knowledge to them by rubbing their hands in the same manner as the woman of the East had done with the "White Men." Hereupon she created two burros, which she gave to the Spanish man and woman. The latter settled down close by. After this, Spider Woman continued to create people in the same manner as she had created the Spaniards, always a man and a woman, giving a different language to each pair. But all at once she found that she had forgotten to create a woman for a certain man, and that is the reason why now there are always some single men.

She continued the creating of people in the same manner, giving new languages as the pairs were formed. All at once she found that she had failed to create a man for a certain woman, in other words, it was found that there was one more woman than there were men. "Oh my!" she said, "How is this?" and then addressing the single woman she said: "There is a single man somewhere, who went away from here. You try to find him and if he accepts you, you live with him. If not, both of you will have to remain single. You do the best you can about that." The two finally found each other, and the woman said, "Where shall we live?" The man answered: "Why here, anywhere. We shall remain together." So he went to work and built a house for them in which they lived. But it did not take very long before they commenced to quarrel with each other. "I want to live here alone," the woman said. "I can prepare food for myself." "Yes, but who will get the wood for you? Who will work the fields?" the man said. "We had better remain together." They made up with each other, but peace did not last. They soon quarreled again, separated for a while, came together again, separated again, and so on. Had these people not lived in that way, all the other Hopi would now live in peace, but others learned it from them, and that is the reason why there are so many contentions between the men and their wives. These were the kind of people that Spider Woman had created. The Huruing Wuhti of the west heard about this and commenced to meditate upon it. Soon she called the goddess from the east to come over again, which the latter did. "I do not want to live here alone," the deity of the west said, "I also want some good people to live here." So she also created a number of other people, but always a man and a wife. They were created in the same manner as the deity of the east had created hers. They lived in the west. Only wherever the people that Spider Woman had created came in contact with these good people there was trouble. The people at that time led a nomadic life, living mostly on game. Wherever they found rabbits or antelope or deer they would kill the game and eat it. This led to a good many contentions among the people. Finally the Woman of the west said to her people: "You remain here; I am going to live, after this, in the midst of the ocean in the west. When you want anything from me, you pray to me there." Her people regretted this very much, but she left them. The Huruing Wuhti of the east did exactly the same thing, and that is the reason why at the present day the places where these two live are never seen.

Those Hopi who now want something from them deposit their prayer offerings in the village. When, they say their wishes and prayers they think of those two who live in the far distance, but of whom the Hopi believe that they still remember them.

The Spanish were angry at Huruing Wuhti and two of them took their guns and proceeded to the abiding place of the deity. The Spaniards are very skillful and they found a way to get there. When they arrived at the house of Huruing Wuhti the latter at once surmised what their intentions were. "You have come to kill me," she said; "don't do that; lay down your weapons and I shall show you something; I am not going to hurt you." They laid down their arms, whereupon she went to the rear end of the kiva and brought out a white lump like a stone and laid it before the two men, asking them to lift it up. One tried it, but could not lift it up, and what was worse, his hands adhered to the stone. The other man tried to assist him, but his hands also adhered to the stone, and thus they were both prisoners. Hereupon Huruing Wuhti took the two guns and said: "These do not amount to anything," and then rubbed them between her hands to powder. She then said to them: "You people ought to live in peace with one another. You people of Spider Woman know many things, and the people whom we have made also know many, but different, things. You ought not to quarrel about these things, but learn from one another; if one has or knows a good thing he should exchange it with others for other good things that they know and have. If you will agree to this I shall release you. They said they did, and that they would no more try to kill the deity. Then the latter went to the rear end of the kiva where she disappeared through an opening in the floor, from where she exerted a secret influence upon the stone and thus released the two men, They departed, but Huruing Wuhti did not fully trust them, thinking that they would return, but they never did.

Coming of the Hopi from the Underworld

Told by Lomavantiwa (Shupaulavi)

A long time ago the people were living below. There were a great many of them, but they were often quarreling with one another. Some of them were very much depraved. They abused the women and the maidens, and that led to very many contentions. So the chiefs, who were worried and angry over this, had a council and concluded that they would try to find another place to live. So they first sent out a bird named Motsni, to find a place of exit from this world. He flew up high but was too weak and returned without having been successful. They then sent the Mocking-bird (Yahpa). He was strong and flew up very high and found a place of exit. Returning, he reported this to the chiefs.

In the meanwhile the chiefs had caused a great flood. Many Balololkongwuus came out of the ground with the water, and a great portion of the people were destroyed. When the Mocking-bird had made his report to the chiefs the latter said: "All right, that is good. We are going away from here." They then announced through the crier that in four days they would leave, and that the women should prepare some food, and after they had eaten on the fourth day they would all assemble at the place right under the opening which the Mocking-bird had found. This was done.

The chiefs then planted a pine-tree (calavi), sang around it, and by their singing made it to grow very fast. It grew up to the opening which the Yahpa had found, and when the chiefs tried and shook it, they found that it was fairly strong, but not strong enough for many people to climb up on, especially its branches, which were very thin. So they planted another kind of pine (lo'oqo), sang around it, and made it also to grow up fast. This tree and its branches was much stronger than the other, but while the first one had grown through the opening, this one did not reach it entirely, its uppermost branches and twigs spreading out sideways before they reached the opening. Hereupon they planted in the same manner a reed (bakavi), which proved to be strong, and also grew through the opening like the calavi. Finally they planted a sunflower (ahkawau), and as it was moist where they planted it, it also grew up very fast and to a great size, its leaves also being very large; but the sunflower did not reach the opening. Its very large disk protruded downward before it reached the opening. The sunflower was covered with little thorns all over.

Now they were done with this.

Hereupon Spider Woman, Pookonghoya, his brother Balo'ongawhoya, and the Mocking-bird that had found the opening, climbed up on the calavi in the order mentioned. After they had emerged through the opening, Pookonghoya embraced the calavi, his brother the reed, both holding them firmly that they should not shake when the people were climbing up. The Mocking-bird sat close by and sang a great many songs, the songs that are still chanted at the Wuwuchim ceremony. Spider Woman was also sitting close by watching the proceedings. Now the people began to climb up, some on the calavi, others on the lo'oqo, still others on the ahkavu and on the bakavi. As soon as they emerged, the Mocking-bird assigned them their places and gave them their languages. To one he would say: "You shall be a Hopi, and that language you shall speak." To another: "You shall be a Navaho, and you shall speak that language. “And to a third: "You shall be an Apache, a Mohave, a Mexican", etc., including the White Man. The language spoken in the underworld had been that of the following Pueblo Indians: Kawahykaka, Akokavi, Katihcha, Kotiyti; these four branches of the Pueblo Indians speaking essentially the same language.

In the under-world the people had been very bad, there being many sorcerers and dangerous people, just like there are in the villages to-day who are putting diseases into the people. Of these Popwaktu, one also found his way out with the others. The people kept coming out, and before they were all out the songs of the Mocking-bird were exhausted. "Hapi! pai shulahti! Now! (my songs) are gone," and at once the people who were still on the ladders commenced returning to the under-world, but a very great many had already come out, an equally large number having remained in the under-world, but the Kik-mongwi from below was with the others that came out of the kiva. The people who had emerged remained around the sipapu, as the opening was, and has ever since been called.

At this time no sun existed and it was dark everywhere. The half-grown son of the Kik-mongwi took sick and died, so they buried him. His father was very angry. "Why has some Powaka come out with us?" he said. "We thought we were living alone and wanted to get away from those dangerous men. That is the reason why we have come out, and now one has come with us." Hereupon he called all the people together and said: "On whose account have I lost my child? I am going to make a ball of this fine com-meal and throw it upward, and on whose head that ball alights, him I shall throw down again through the sipapu." Hereupon he threw the ball upward to a great height, the people all standing and watching. When it came down it fell upon the head of some one and was shattered. "Ishohi! so you are the one," the chief said to him. But as it happened this was the chief's nephew (his younger sister's son). "My nephew, so you are nukpana (dangerous); why have you come out with us? We did not want any bad ones here, and now you have come with us. I am going to throw you back again." So he grabbed him in order to throw him back. "Wait," he said, "wait! am going to tell you something." "I am going to throw you back," the chief replied. "Wait," his nephew said again, "until I tell you some thing. You go there to the sipahpuni and you look down. There he is walking." "No, he is not," the chief replied, "I am not going to look down there, he is dead." But he went and looked down and there he saw his boy running around with other children, still showing the signs of the head washing which the Hopi practice upon the dead immediately after death. "Yes, it is true, it is true," the chief said, "truly there he is going about." "So do not throw me down there," his nephew said, "that is the way it will be. If any one dies he will go down there. Let me remain with you, I am going to tell you some more." Then the chief consented and let his nephew remain.

It was still dark, and as there was no sunshine it was also cold, and the people began to look for fire and for wood, but as it was so dark, they could find very little wood. They thus lived there a while without fire, but all at once they saw a light in the distance and the chief said: "Some one go there and see about it." When they had still been in the lower world they had occasionally heard footsteps of some one up above. So some one went in search of the light, but before he had reached it he became tired and returned. Another was sent and he got there. He found a field in which corn, watermelons, beans, etc., were planted. All around this field a fire was burning, which was kept up by wood, and by which the ground was kept warm so that the plants could grow. The messenger found a very handsome man there. He had four strands of turquoise around his neck and very large turquoise ear pendants. In his face he had two black lines running from the upper part of his nose to his cheeks, and made with specular iron. By his side was standing his friend (a mask) which looked very ugly, with large open eye-holes and a large mouth. So it was Skeleton (Masauwuu) whom they had heard walking about from the other world. "Who are you?" Skeleton asked the messenger. "Where do you come from?" "Yes," he replied, "we have come from below, and it is cold here. We are freezing and we have no fire.

"You go and tell your people and then you all come here to me." So he returned and the people asked him: "Now, what have you found out? Have you found anybody?" "Yes," he said, "I have found somebody and he has a good crop there." Skeleton had fed the messenger with some of his good things which he had there. The people had not brought much food with them from below and so they had not very much left. The people were very glad for this invitation and went to the place where Skeleton lived. But when they saw the small field they thought: "Well, that will be gone in a very short time," but Skeleton always planted and the food was never gone. When they came there they gathered some wood and built a fire and then they warmed themselves and were happy. Skeleton gave them roasting ears, and watermelons, melons, squashes, etc., and they ate and refreshed themselves. Some of the plants were very small yet, others still larger, so that they always had food.

So the people remained there, made fields, and they always kept up a fire near the fields, which warmed the ground so that they could raise a crop. When the crop had matured they gathered it all in, and when they now had provisions they planned to start off again, but there was still no sun, and it was cold. So they talked about this, saying: "Now, it ought not remain this way." So the chiefs all met in council with Skeleton, and talked this matter over in order to see whether they could not make a sun as they had had it in the underworld, but they did not just know how to do it. So they finally took a piece of dressed buffalo hide (hakwavu), which they cut in a round shape, stretched it over a wooden ring, and then painted it with white du'ma (kaoline). They then pulverized some black paint (toho) with which they drew a picture of the moon around the edge of this disk, sprinkling the center of the disk with the same black color. They then attached a stick to this disk. Hereupon they stretched a large piece of white native cloth (mochapu) on the floor and placed this disk on it. All these objects they had brought with them from the under-world.

They then selected some one (the story does not say whom) and directed him to stand on this moon symbol. Hereupon the chiefs took the cloth by it, corners, swung it back and forth, and then threw it upward, where it continued swiftly flying eastward into the sky. So the people sat and watched. All at once they noticed that it became light in the east. Something was burning there as they thought. The light became brighter and brighter, and something came up in the east. It rose higher and higher, and where the people were it became lighter and lighter. So now they could go about and they were happy. That turned out to be the moon, and though it was light, the light was only dim and the people, when working in the fields, would still occasionally cut off their plants because they could not see very distinctly, and it was still cold and the people were freezing, and they still had to keep the ground warm with fires. So the people were thinking about it. The chiefs again met in council, and said: "Ishohi! It is better already, it is light, but it is not quite good yet. It is still cold. Can we not make something better?" They concluded that perhaps the buffalo skin was not good, and that it was too cold, so they decided that this time they would take a piece of mochapu. They again cut out a round piece, stretched it over a ring, but this time painted it with oxide of copper (cakwa). They painted eyes and a mouth on the disk, and decorated the forehead of what this was to resemble in yellow, red, and other colors. They put a ring of corn-husks around it, which were worked in a zigzag fashion. Around this they tied a tawahona, that is, a string of red horse-hair, finally thrusting a number of eagle-tail feathers into a corn-husk ring, fastened to the back of the disk. In fact, they prepared a sun symbol as it is still worn on the back of the flute players in the Flute ceremony. To the forehead of the face painted on the disk they tied an abalone shell. Finally the chief made nakwakwosis of the feathers of a small yellowish bird, called irahoya, which resembles a fly-catcher, but has some red hair on top of the head.

Of these nakwakwosis the chief tied one to the point of each eagle-tail feather on the sun symbol. They then placed this symbol on the white cloth again, again asked some one to stand on it, and, as in the case of the moon, they swung the cloth with its contents into the air, where it kept twirling upward and upward towards the east. Soon they again saw a light rise in the east. It became brighter and brighter and warmer. That proved to be the sun, and it had not come up very high when the Hopi already felt its warmth. After the sun had been created and was rising day after day, the people were very happy, because it was now warm and very light, so that they could attend to their work very well. The children were running around and playing. They were now thinking of moving on. They had a great many provisions by this time, and so the chiefs again met in a council to talk the matter over. "Let us move away from here," the chiefs said; "let us go eastward and see where the sun rises, but let us not go all together. Let some take one route, others another, and others still further south, and then we shall see who arrives at the place where the sun rises first. So the people started. The White People took a southern route, the Hopi a more northern, and between them traveled what are now the Pueblo Indians of New Mexico. Often certain parties would remain at certain places, sometimes for several years. They would build houses and plant.

Soon they became estranged from each other, and would begin to attack and kill one another. The Castilians were especially bad, and made wars on other people. When starting, the chiefs had agreed that as soon as one of the parties should reach the place where the sun rises, many stars would fall from the sky, and when that would happen all the traveling parties should remain and settle down where they would be at that time. The White People having taken a southern route, were more gifted than the other people. When they had become very tired carrying their children and their burdens, one of the women bathed herself and took the scales that she had rubbed off from her body and made horses of these scales. These horses they used after that for traveling, so that they could proceed very much faster. In consequence of this they arrived at the place where the sun rises before any of the other parties arrived there. And immediately many stars fell from the sky. "Aha!" the people said who were still traveling; "Some one has already arrived." Hereupon they settled down where they were. It had also been agreed upon before the different parties started, that whenever those who did not reach the place where the sun rises should be molested by enemies, they should notify those who had arrived at the sunrise, and the latter, would then come and help them.

The Origin of Some Oraibi Clans

Told by Wikvaya (Oraibi)

Away down the sipapu in the under-world the people lived in the same manner as they do here. The wife of the chief of the Bear clan often danced in the Butterfly dance (Polihtikivee), at which the chief got angry. The Spider clan had also a chief. The Bear chief sent the Po'okong to limit for them another life (katci) or world and see whether they could not get out. He was so angry at his wife's participating in the dance, fearing that she would be led astray, he wanted to go away and leave her.

Po'okong and his younger brother Balo'ongahoya went in search of another world, and when they returned, reported that there was an opening right above them. Po'okong had reached it by means of a reed on which he had spit and thus made it strong. The chief said, as they were still dancing (the Butterfly dance) they would move in four days. After four days they were still dancing, and the chief said to some one that he would not tell his wife anything, but try to find another wife. So he left, being accompanied by Po'okong and, Balo'ongahoya, the Polis still dancing wildly. They started and went out, Po'okong first, then Balo'ongahoya, then the Bear clan chief, who was followed by the Spider clan chief. Then the Bear clan people, the Spider clan people, and after them many other people came out. When many were out the Bear chief closed the opening. When they were out the chief said, "Well, what now?" They were in the dark yet, the entrance, however, being closed. The chief sent the Eagle who flew around hunting an opening or light. H returned, and the chief asked: "Taa um hin nawoti?" "Well, I found an opening and made it more light, but it is very hot high up yet. Send another one." So the chief sent the Buzzard (Wicoko). The latter ascended higher but got burned (hence he has no feathers on his head and wings), but he made it lighter, When he returned that chief said: "Thank you. Well, now what? Now it is somewhat better. The sky has been opened somewhat more and it is much lighter." The question arose: Which way? The Bear clan spoke for the South, the Spider clan for the north, and the latter talking more and getting the greater crowd, the Spider clan went northward.

The Spider Clan

This clan traveled northward. The chief first, the people following. After four nights they carne to a nice country, where the "North Old Man" (Kwinae Wuhtaka) lives. But it was cold there.

The chief decided that there they would stay. So the people were glad and began to plant corn, watermelon, melons, sweet corn, etc. The chief had brought with him the cult and altar of the Blue Flutes. When the corn began to grow the chief put up his altar, sang and fluted, but he did all that alone. So the corn, etc., grew nicely, but when it tasseled and the ears began to develop, it became cold and the crop was destroyed. "Ishohi!" (Oh!) the people exclaimed.

They tried it another year, but the same: thing was repeated in every respect. Again no crop. Another year it was tried, but now the corn only began to tassel, and the fourth year it was still very small when the frost killed it. Then there was dissatisfaction. "Ishohi! (Oh!) Our Father, you have spoken falsely, you said it was good here." So they all also started southward after the Bear People.

After the first night the chief said to his wife: "You bathe yourself." This she did (in warm water). Then she rubbed her body and collected the small scales which she had rubbed from her skin and handed them to her husband. He laid them on a blanket until there was a considerable quantity of them. He then wrapped this in a reed receptacle, sang over it and waved it four times, whereupon the scales turned into burros and rushed out. "What is that?" the people asked. "Those are burros," the chief said. So they were glad that now they would not have to carry everything themselves any longer, and the chief said that now they would move on towards the rising sun.

The chief and his wife repeated the same performance, but instead of burros, Spaniards came out. To them the chief said: You put supplies and your things on the burros and follow the other Hopi (that is, the Bear clan), and when you overtake them, kill them. So the Castilians went south, and the Spider people went south-east, following a Stream (Nono'pbaya, a rolling stream, because of the high recoiling waves). They came to a nice place where they stayed one year and planted and reaped a crop. From there they proceeded south-east, stopped another year at a certain place, where they again planted, but were harassed by enemies. They saved a portion of the crop and proceeding farther south-east they ascended a bluff or mesa, staying another year and planting in the valleys.

Thus they stopped in all at ten different places, but being constantly harassed by the people along the water, they never planted more than once. Finally they arrived where the sun rises and the Americans (Bahanas) live. With them they became friends; here they planted, their children learned the language a little, and they stayed there three years. They also here learned that the Bear clan had been there and had already gone westward again. The Spider people followed, arrived at Oraibi, where they found, the Bear clan, whom they joined. Their chief was then Machito. They also had the A'ototo and Aholi Katcinas.

The Bear Clan

This clan had gone south from the sipahpuni. They had with them the A'ototo Katcina. They soon found the Young Corn Ear (Pihk'ash) people with the Aholi Katcina, who wanted to join them. So the Bear clan chief took them along. They stopped at a place and here had a good crop because they had the two Katcinas with them. The next year they came to a clear stream. In all they stopped ten times before arriving at the Americans, where the sun rises. Here they stopped four years. Their children learned a little English. The land being scarce, the Americans told them to go west and hunt land for themselves, and if anybody would be bad to them (nukpana) and cause their children to die, they (the Americans) would come and cut the Nukapana's heads off. This was told them, because they (the Americans) had been told that down in the old home there had been Popwaktu (sorcerers, etc.). So they traveled westward, found the Pueblo, but no good land that they could get. So they finally arrived at Shongopavi, where some people lived, and there they settled down.

One time the people saw that the chief, Machito, held a sweet corn-ear between every two fingers, at the same time eating from the other hand. Corn was very scarce at that time, so the people spoke to him about his greediness, at which he got angry and left, taking with him the A'ototo and Aholi. Hunters later found them at a rock, now Bean Spreading Place (Bahpu-Moyanpi), where there is still a stone on which there is some writing called Machitutubeni. Machito left his wife at Shongopavi, also his people, who then formed the Shongopavi Bear clan. When the hunters found him they informed the people at Shongopavi.

Some went there to get them back, but Machito would not listen to them. Then his wife went to him but he would not listen to her either. So they left him. Machito took a big stone and went with them for some distance to make the landmark between Oraibi and Shongopavi. The people said several times: "Put it here." But he would not listen until arriving at a place called "Ocapchomo," where he placed it, thus making a landmark between the fields of the Shongopavi and his own.

Then Machito and the two Katcinas went up the Oraibi mesa where they remained. Later the Spider people arrived. Machito asked about their wanderings and they told him. He wanted to know why the corn would not grow although they had the Flute cult. The Spider clan chief accused the "North Old Man." Machito then said: "All right, you may live here, but as your cult does not seem to be effective, you watch the sun for me, and when he has arrived at his south limit, you tell me, and we shall have the Soyal ceremony. Also your pu'htavi does not seem to have been good, so I want you to make my kind of pu'htavi."

After the matter had been settled between Machito and the Spider clan chief, the latter's people came up. Among these were also the Lizard clan, to which the Sand clan is related. These names were given to people while wandering. One would find and see something, perhaps under peculiar circumstances, and he called after it. The Lizard people were also asked what they knew and when they said the

Marau cult, they were also permitted to stay, but were requested to co-operate in the Soyal ceremony. For that reason Pungnanomsi, who is of the Bear clan, and village chief, now makes the puhu (road) in the night of the Marau ceremony from the natsi at the south end of the kiva towards the rising sun.

The Rattle-snake (Tcu'a) clan also came with the Spider clan to Oraibi, but it is not known how or where this clan became a part of the Spider clan, The Badger people understand medicines, hence they prepare the medicine--for instance, charm liquid--for the Flute, Snake, Marau, and other ceremonies.

Another Badger clan and the Butterfly (Powul) came from Kishi-wuu. These brought the Powamu and Katcina cult.

The Divided Spring (Batki) clan came from where the sun rises.

They came to the village of Oraibi and arranged a contest at Muyiovatki where each planted corn, the Blue Flutes sweet corn, the others, Wupakao, over which they played the whole day. The sweet corn grew first, and so the Blue Flutes to this day go to the village in processions, etc., first closing the well (batni) on the plaza. Later the Drab Flutes (Masitalentu) had to throw their meal, mollas, etc., from a distance to the warrior (Kelehtaka) of the Cakwalalentu, who put them into the well in the booth for them.

The Wanderings of the Spider Clan (Kohk'ang-Namu)

Told by Tawiima (Mishongnovi)

In the under-world many people became very bad. They had many contentions, and began to kill the people and also killed the chief's son; so the chief concluded that they would move away from there. But the question was, how to get out?' So he sent the Motsni to find a place where they could get out. He flew up and found an opening, and came back and reported the same to the chief. So the Village Chief (Kik-mongwi) and the Crier Chief (Chaak-mongwi) planted a pine (calavi), which grew up very fast, but did not quite reach the opening. They then planted a reed (bakavi) which also grew up fast and reached through the opening. On this reed they climbed till, first the Horn people (Aaltu), who then stood outside and held the protruding part of the reed or ladder. Many people then followed.

The Mocking-bird (Yahpa) was sitting outside and distributed the languages to the People. As they were climbing up one of them dropped one of his moccasins. Below the Hopi had pretty moccasins, but as this moccasin was dropped and the man had to make another one, and could not make it as nicely as the other one had been, the Hopi now have not very nice moccasins. The people had not yet all come out when the chief stopped them and

closed up the opening, but one of the sorcerers (Popwaktu) had also come out.
From here the people now started on different routes, the White Man taking the most southern route. All the other people took different routes further north. The 'Hopi brought with them Mu'yingwu, whose body consisted entirely of corn, his feet being ears of corn, so that he could not move very fast. The Hopi were to have the horse, but as they tried to ride him they could not do so, as they did not put any bridle on him; so the Navaho, wearing a band around their head, tried it and they could ride him. The two matched together better for that reason because they also bridled the pony, probably with yucca leaves.

They had not gone very far when the chief's son took sick and died. They thought that the sorcerer who was with them had killed him, but the latter said: "Nobody has died, he is not dead; just go and look down into the opening through which we came. He is down there." So the chief went and looked down there, and beheld his child walking about in the other world. So they took the Powaku with them. He said that hereafter no one would be really dead, but the people who would die would simply go back to the lower world. After they had travelled for some time, just how long tradition does not say, the Coyote who had carried the stars in his hand, and was traveling with the Hopi people, threw the stars into the sky so that from that time it was somewhat light during the night.

The White People had taken with them the Spider which was very skillful, so that when they had traveled some distance the Spider rubbed some scales from her skin, and from these created burros. These the White Men afterwards used for carrying their burdens. So they got along faster and reached the place where the sun rises first. When they arrived there a star arose in the south, which told the other migrating people that some one had arrived at the sunrise. This was a signal that they had agreed upon before starting. This star is said to have influence over the animals, and the old people say that whoever wants to own a horse, cattle, sheep, etc., should pray to this star, which the Hopi are doing to this day.

So the people traveled on. All at once one party came upon a bear that had died there. They were called the Bear (Honawu) clan. Right after them came another party, who cut straps from the skin of the bear and were called Piqosha clan, the name given by the Hopi to this peculiar strap. Another party followed and found the cadaver covered with spider web, from which they were called Spider (Kohk'ang) clan. A fourth party found blue-birds sitting on the cadaver and they were called the Blue-bird (Choro) clan. A fifth party found that maggots had eaten out the eyes, leaving the cavities bare with a little fat still attached to the bone. From this they were called Fat Cavity clan (Wikorzh-namu). A sixth migrating party came upon the scene and found that a mole had dug his way up under the place where the cadaver had been lying, and hence they were called Mole (Mu'yi) clan. Here the parties who had thus received their clan names soon separated, and the Spider clan after this wandered about and stopped at various places for a long time. The other clans did the same, living shorter or longer periods at one place, which accounts for the many smaller and larger ruins with which the country is covered.

Finally the Spider clan arrived at a spring (about four miles north of the present village sites of Mishongnovi and Shupaulavi) called Homiqopu. Here they remained for some time, there still being ruins at that place. From here this clan moved to a place about a mile northeast of Shupaulavi, called Chukuvi. At the foot of the mesa on which this village was situated was a very large spring. The Squash (Batanga) clan then ruled in this village, the chief belonging to that clan. The Sand (Tuwa) clan was also one of the clans being numerous in the village at that time. The inhabitants of the different villages were often harassed by enemies, among them the Utes and Apache. It seems that even the inhabitants of the different villages often made raids on each other. For this reason the inhabitants of Chukuvi and those of old Mishongnovi, which was situated, however, west of its present location, way down the mesa, moved on the mesa and built the present village of Mishongnovi.

In Mishongnovi the Blue-bird clan was then in charge of the village, the chief belonging to that clan, but it seems that this clan, shared the chieftainship with the following clans, which furnished the Kik-mongwi, the Village Chief, in the order named, for four year, a new chief being elected every four years: After the Blue-bird clan followed the Bear clan, then the Batki clan, and lastly, the Squash clan, The Sand clan, having lived in the village of Chukuvi, is said to have moved to Oraibi, east of which village they had had fields while they were still living at Chukuvi. At the time when the people lived at Chukuvi, Shupaulavi was also inhabited, but it seems that the people then, too, lived farther down, probably at the so-called First Ledge, but when Mishongnovi was built the people of Shupaulavi also moved on to the top of the mesa.

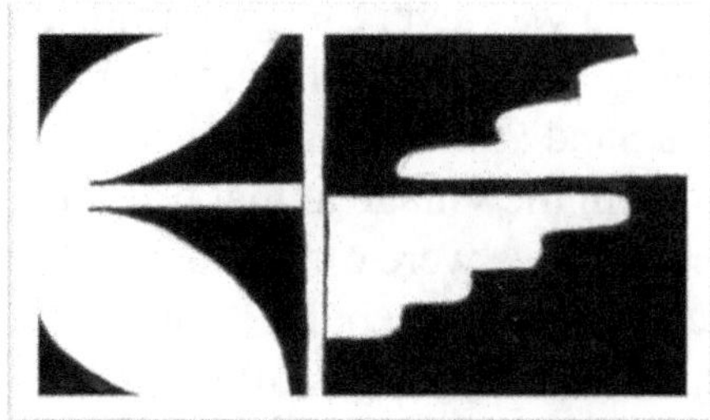

The Origin of the Yayaatu Society

Told by Wikvaya (Oraibi)

Ishyaoi! In Oraibi they were living. In the home of the Reed clan lived the Yayaa-mongwi. This Fraternity has now died out, but its altar paraphernalia are still kept in the house. A long time ago a man and his wife had one little boy. Some children of the village would often visit this boy. They were lazy, though their parents often told them to work, and get wood, herd sheep, etc. They would not listen, but often assembled at this house where they would prepare some food in the corners in front of the house, having stolen the food in the village. In a corner in front of the house they would build their fire, the wood they stole from the different houses in the village. So the men in the village were very angry at them and so were the mothers of these children. "You are lazy," they often told them. "You do not want to work, and we are not going to feed you." So they would go and steal some food in the houses and eat that.

One time the priest's son suggested to the others: "Let us go and get some wood ourselves. Some one go and steal a hide strap (piqo'sha) somewhere." So after they had eaten they went through the village and gathered up piqo'shas of different lengths and returned. They left the village on the east, drank at K'eqo'chmovi, and then went farther east and gathered some dry brush in the valley. After they had all gathered their bundles the priest's son said: "Are you all done?" "Yes," they said. "All right, then let us go home now," he said. But just when they were ready to start a Hawk in the form of a man carne upon them. He wore many strands of beads around his neck and had a black line painted with specular iron running over his nose down to the cheeks. The hair of all of the children was very much disheveled, so he laughed at them. "Are you getting wood?" he said. "Yes," they replied, and he again laughed at them.

His kiva was close by. "You come in here," he said to the children, so they went in. It was a kiva just like those in the village. He invited them to sit down on the banquette that ran along the wall, so they sat down. He then took a seat near the fire-place, filled a pipe and took two puffs from it. He then said to the children that they should take a seat near the fireplace, too. He handed the pipe first to the priest's son, who smoked, addressing the man as "My father" (Inaa), which pleased the man very much. All then smoked, one after another, all exchanging terms of relationship, the older ones addressing the younger ones, "My younger brother," and the younger ones the older ones as "My older brother." He then said to them that they should remain, as he was going to feed them, and after having eaten they might go home.

Hereupon he went into another room and brought back a large roll of qo'mi (a bread made of the meal of roasted sweet corn-ears) which he fed to them. After they had eaten he went into another chamber and brought forth a large roll of kilts, eagle wing feathers (kwavok'i), ear pendants, eagle breath feathers, to be tied into the hair, beads, etc., and handed all these to the children. Hereupon he dressed up all the boys, tying the kilts behind. He then handed an eagle feather to each one and directed them to stand in a line. Hereupon Kish Taka, the Hawk-man, took a mo'chapu, which is a native cloth or owa, wrapped it up, and holding it under his left arm, took a stand at the south end of the line, saving to the youths: "Now then, whatever you see me do, you do the same." Hereupon he commenced to go around the kiva crying, "Ow" (long drawn). They went around in a circle in the kiva four times emitting the same sounds at short intervals. Hereupon he went up the ladder, the youths following him. Outside he again told them to do as they would see him do. He jumped off the kiva, ran about through the brush, the youths always following him and all constantly saying. "Ow, ow." Suddenly he threw down the mo'chapu, spreading it on the ground, grabbed the priest's son, threw him on the cloth, and then asked the other youths to take a hold of the cloth at different places and in this way they carried the priest's son to the kiva, throwing him through the opening into the kiva.

Hereupon they waited, and in a little while the youth came out of the kiva again, unharmed. Hereupon he grabbed another of the youths and they threw him down, and in this same manner every one was thrown into the kiva and came out unharmed. Then the Hawk-man went into the kiva, being followed by all of the youths. He was called the uncle of the youths. After they had entered the kiva he drew aside a curtain from one of the inner chambers and in the room behind the curtain were four round ovens (koici) dug into the earth, in which an old woman kept up a fire. The Hawk-man then grabbed the priest's son, threw him into one of the ovens, the old woman spurting some medicine on him as he fell in. Hereupon the other youths were thrown into the ovens. As soon as the costumes were burned off the bodies, the Hawk-man took them out again and placed all the, bodies north of the fireplace in the kiva, and covered them with the aforementioned piece of native cloth. When this was done he sat down and sang a song over the bodies. Soon the bodies under the cloth began to move and the priest's son was the first to come out, the others following soon, all now being alive again.

Hereupon he told them to sit down on the banquette on the west side of the kiva. The old woman now came out and washed the heads of the youths, giving a perfect white ear of corn (chochmingwuu) to each one. The Hawk hereupon addressed them, saying: "Thanks, that you are now done. You are now prepared. You can go home now. Take your wood to the Blue Flute (Cakwalanvi) kiva, and enter that kiva and remain there. Do not go into the houses to get something to eat, but wait for me there. After sundown I shall come to you." Hereupon he handed an eagle wing feather (kwavok'i) to the priest's son, whereupon the youths left.

When they came with their bundles of wood to the Blue Flute kiva the people saw them and said: "Aha! the lazy boys have gotten their own wood. Now maybe they will not steal any more." When they had put down their wood, they ran to the houses where they had gotten the burden straps and threw them on and into the houses, without, however, entering them. They all returned to the kiva at once without having partaken of any food. The sun had now gone down. They waited awhile and after the evening dawn had disappeared and it was quite dark they heard somebody come. It was the Hawk, in whose kiva they had been, and he at once entered the kiva. "Are you all sitting here?" the Hawk asked. "Yes, we are all here. Sit down," the youths replied. So the Hawk took a seat near the fireplace and at once filled a pipe and they all smoked.

The Hawk had brought with him a small bowl and some kwiptoci (meal from white corn that has first been soaked and then popped). Of this meal he made a gruel in the bowl, which he fed to the youths.

He then told them that they should not go home, but early in the morning some of them should take a seat in the north end of the kiva and the others in the south end of the kiva. The first should be fire jumpers (Tovuchochoyanik'am) and also Yayaatus. The others should be the singers (Tataok'am). Between the two parties he sprinkled a meal line on the floor of the kiva. One he selected to act as watchman. He should keep up the fires at the fireplace and keep out intruders. He told them that they should remain in a sitting posture in the kiva all of the next day and that they should fast all day. In the evening he would return and feed them again. Thus they were assembled here in the kiva, and each one had his "mother" (his white corn-ear) standing against the wall by his side. The people were wondering the next day why the little thieves, as they called them, were not coming out to hunt something to eat. Finally one of the women approached the kiva, looked in, and saw them sitting in an erect posture. "Oh," she said to the people, "they are assembled (yu'ngiota) in there."

They remained in this way in the kiva for four days, their uncle coming every night to feed them and look after them. Early in the morning after the fourth clay he washed their heads. The following day it was Totokya (a name always applied to the day preceding a ceremony). In the evening of this day the Hawk-man brought with him the costumes for the youths, consisting of kilts, beads, eagle feathers, twisted yarn (naalongmurukpu), ear pendants, ankle bands, and also some yellow paint (sik'ahpik'i). All these he placed on the floor north of the fireplace. During the night the youth who had been watching the fireplace in the kiva dug four ovens on the plaza south-west of the kiva, while the others buried a long cotton string in the ground on the same plaza. They also stretched long strings along the houses of the village, pasting them to the walls with qo'mi dough. Early in the morning the watcher of the kiva went around through the village begging for some wood. With this he heated the four ovens on the plaza. The people wondered what he was going to do, some suggesting that perhaps he was going to bake some pikami (a food prepared in small ovens outside of the houses for festal occasions).

While this youth was beating the ovens the Hawk dressed up all the others in the kiva. He painted a wide yellow band from shoulder to shoulder running down over the chest; the lower arms and lower legs he also painted yellow, and a yellow ring around the abdomen. Their faces he covered with corn-pollen. They had many strands of beads and also some strands of the twisted yarn consisting of dark blue and brownish red yarn. Large bunches of eagle feathers were tied to the top of their heads, and an eagle tale feather was tied on each side of their head in such a manner that their points extended backward. From these tail feathers were also suspended strands of the twisted yarn. Old Hopi Women's belts were tied over the kilts. Strands of the same yarn were tied around their wrists.

At about noon the singers came out first, each one throwing a pinch of sacred meal towards the sun. The Hawk-man and the old woman remained in the kiva. As soon as the singers had emerged from the kiva they went with long strides to the plaza (the same where now the Snake dance takes place) where they lined up and sang.

As soon as they had formed in line the Yayaatu also emerged from the kiva and went to the plaza with long strides, the priest's son carrying this time the mochapu which the Hawk-man had used when initiating the youths. While the first party continued singing, the Yayaatu rummaged through the village, ascending the roofs of the houses, jumping onto the people, tearing up and throwing down chimneys, taking hold of children and people and swinging them over the edge of the roof and threatening to throw them down, etc. The people got very angry at them and beat them with sticks, so they finally returned to the plaza. Arriving there, the priest's son, now the leading priest of this order, banding the mochapu to one of the others, jumped into one of the ovens. The others drew him out dead, wrapped him up in the mochapu, took him to the kiva and threw him into it. Here he was at once resuscitated by the Hawk-man and the old woman and came up apparently unharmed, having on again the same costume as the one that had been burned off his body in the oven. While this was going on, others had jumped into the various ovens and were drawn out immediately, thrown into the kiva, and treated the same way.

By this time the parents and relatives of these youths became very much alarmed and began to cry and complain that their children were killed that way, but the young man that had been watching the kiva told them not to come near, saying that they were going to have a dance yet. After they were through with this performance, their leader went into the kiva and brought out a mochapu, in which he had something wrapped up. This he placed on the ground on the plaza and all the Yayaatu crowded around this bundle. Covering another large mochapu over them, they occupied themselves for a short time with the bundle. They then threw off the covering and standing in a circle around the bundle they sang. In a little while they opened the bundle and there were many fine, large watermelons in it. Leaving these watermelons on the plaza, the leader again went into the kiva, brought out another bundle, over and around which they went through the same performance. Uncovering this bundle a great many little cotton-tail rabbits jumped up, which they distributed among the children. The singers kept up their singing during all these performances.

The Yayaatu now all entered the kiva. Soon they came out again, some hunting and uncovering the strings that they had buried and attached to the houses. Others that followed them wound the strings up on balls. Whenever one string was found and wound up, another one was hunted and wound, so they all went through the village hunting and winding the strings that they had buried. Suddenly they all proceeded to the house of the Cotton-tall Rabbit clan (Tab-namu), where Homihoiniwa and his family now live, and here one of the strings ran into a water-jug. This they lifted up without drawing the string out, and carried it also to the plaza where they split it in two. It was found that on the inside a cloud symbol was painted in each half jug. They lifted up the two parts of the jug and showed the cloud symbols to the people. Hereupon they covered up the two parts, sang over them, and when they took the covering off the jug was whole again as before, whereupon they returned it to the house.

The leader once more went into the kiva and came back with a bowl containing some diluted white kaolin (dumakuyi). This they took to the top of the Marau kiva, which is so situated that from it a long high bluff, which is called Canavitoika, can be plainly seen in the distance (probably eight or ten miles to the west). The Yayaatu now gathered around the bowl and putting eagle feathers into the white kaolin they moved them up and down in the air, as if whitewashing that distant bluff, and behold, the bluff, though far away, at once assumed a white color. All the people could plainly see that it was being whitewashed, though it is far away. Hereupon they returned to the plaza, the singers now stopping their singing. They cut up the watermelons and distributed slices. All then entered the kiva again, the mothers and the relatives of these youths now crowding towards this kiva wanting to get their children. The watcher of the kiva kept them back, saying, however, that they had not yet been discharmed.

When they had all entered the kiva the Hawk-man discharmed them and then set no'ekwiwi and white piki before them, saying: "Now eat and then you sleep in the kiva one night. In the morning when your people come for you, you can go with them." In the evening the mothers again came and clamored for their children, but the youth, that was watching the kiva, told them to go home, as they were going to sleep there one night. The Hawk-man and the old woman then wrapped up all the costumes and other paraphernalia returned to their kiva in the valley east of the village. Only the corn-ear mothers they left for each one. In the morning the youths all went to their homes, and after that they were no longer bad and dangerous. They formed the Yayaatu Society and directed their prayers towards the place where their uncle, the Hawk-man, lived, and where they had been initiated.

The Origin of Some Mishongnovi Clans

Told by Sik'anakpu (Mishongnovi)

The Batki clan and the Sand clan come from Palatkwapi. When traveling, the Sand clan would spread sand on the ground and plant corn. The Batki clan would cause it to thunder and rain (by singing), the crop would grow in a day and they would have something to eat. At Homolovi (Winslow) they lived a long time. They brought with them the Soyal cult, the Lagon cult, and the Soyal Katcina. They went to Aoatovi. Here they were not welcome, and hence moved on to Mishongnovi, where they found the Bear, Parrot and Crow clans. They were asked what they knew to produce rain and crops. They spread the sand, made corn grow, etc., whereupon they were welcomed and their leader was made the chief of the village.

The spring Toriva was then very small. But the Batki-namu had brought from the Little Colorado River mud, grass, and water in a mongwikuru. This they put into the spring and that increased the flow of the water, and there was also much grass around it formerly, when there were fewer burros than there are now. The Bear clan had the Antelope cult, the Parrot and the Crow clans the Blue Flute cult. The Crane and the Eagle clans had the position of the village crier, and the Drab Flute cult. The Batki were admitted to the Antelope and Blue Flute Fraternities, and hence Sik'anakpu makes the cloud symbols in the ceremony of the Blue Flute society.

After that the Young Corn-Ear (Pihk'ash) or Corn-Ear (Kao') clan came from the east, from the Pueblo,

Sik'anakpu thinks. According to Sik'anakpu the earlier clans came to Mishongnovi as follows:

The Parrot and Crow clans, who had the Blue Flute cult and the village chief.

The Bear clan, who brought the Antelope altar now used in the Snake ceremony.

The Crane and Eagle clan brought the Drab Flute and Marau cult, and had the village crier.

The Katcina clan, with the Katcinas.

The Sand clan, with the Lagon, Soyal, and Snake cult.

The Batki clan. These had no cult, but controlled the water.

The Young Corn-Ear clan. These had no special cult, but brought a better quality of corn.

Before the Batki people came, the corn was very small. They made it rain and so it grew large. The Pihk'ash clan brought better and larger corn with them.

The Destruction of Palatkwapi

Told by Lomavantiwa (Shupaulavi)

After all the people, except the Zunis, had come out from the underworld through the sipahpuni, they remained for some time with Skeleton (Masauwuu). When they were traveling eastward from here on different routes, and in different sections and parties, a large party came to a place called Palatkwapi, somewhere south-east of Flagstaff, in southern Arizona. Among these were the Divided Water clan (Batki-namu).

So these people had their clan name before they arrived at the above -mentioned place, but with them a great many other people stopped at Palatkwapi. Here they remained for a long time, for the truth of which statement the extensive ruins at that place are proof. The name seems to be derived from a high bluff of red stone. The people, especially the young men, here became very bad. They ill-treated the people sometimes in a disgraceful manner. One time a young man again shamefully mistreated an old man, who then became very angry. This old man belonged to the Batki clan. He went and reported the same to the village chief (Kik-mongwi), crier chief (Chaak-mongwi) and the warrior chief (Kalehtak-mongwi), so they assembled in the old man's house and asked him what was the matter, why he had called them. "Yes," the old man answered, "these young men here are very bad, they treat one very mean when one goes to the rear, and I am angry at them, so I called you here to tell you about it, what you think about it." So they talked the matter over and the village chief said: "We shall move away from here." So he called his son and told him: "You run to a distant place, Pine Ridge (Loqo'nmuru). So the young man ran and when he came back his father asked him: "How is it now, are you strong?" "Yes," the son replied, "my legs are strong now." "All right," the father said. Both of them were sorcerers (Powaka), bad men.

Hereupon the father dressed four masks for him: the mask of the Yahponcha, the La'nang Katcina, Aha Katcina (Oraibi: Kuruwa), and the Katcin-mana. The first resembles that of Skeleton (Masauwuu), only it had small bunches of hair on each side and in front. All these masks the young man put on his head, first that of the Mana, secondly the La'nang Katcina mask, thirdly the Aha mask, and lastly that of the Yahponcha. The father had dressed them during the night. He then strung a number of fingers which he had cut off of old dry corpses, and tied them to both of his son's wrists as rattles. He furthermore prepared a long cedar-bark fuse which he handed to the young man. After he had thus dressed his son, the chief said: "Now you run back to Pine Ridge and set the pine timber there on fire, then you come back here." The son did as he had been told and coming back he climbed up to the house of his father. He now acted as a Ghost (dualangwu). The people had not noticed his going or coming. After he had arrived in the house he ground corn on his sister's small mealing stone. While he was grinding he sang: "Tu'tawunaha! tu'tawunaha!"

Hereupon he left the house and again ran away and set other timbers on fire.

The next night he returned, again ground a little corn, and departed. This time the people became suspicious, and when they assembled in their kivas in the morning they inquired who had been about. They said: "Some one had gone into the house of the chief and ran away again," and they requested some young men to hide away the next night and watch. By this time several fires could be seen in the distant timbers. The next night a number of young men watched, hiding away at the different corners of the village, and one also in the recess of the plaza. During the night the Powaka again lighted several fires in the timbers and came rushing into the village. When he arrived there his fuse had gone out, but they saw him enter into the village and ascend into the house of the village chief, where they heard him grinding and singing again. He again immediately left the house and passed one of the watchers, the latter jumping up, but the ghost dashed by, springing across the plaza, where the watcher became so scared that he did not make himself known, but remained in a crouching position, So he dashed away and lighted other fires.

In the morning they talked the matter over in. the kivas, saying to the watchers: "You are of no account. Next night we shall watch again, many of us." They agreed that they would watch at different places, one also taking a position on the path that led down from the village through a river or creek that passed by. So during the night many watchers were distributed and hid away in the corners and recesses of the streets, a weakly young man, an orphan, taking a position near the aforesaid path at the river. They again noticed the fires in the woods and all at once saw the ghost running towards the village again, crossing the plaza, and running up the ladder of the village chief's house. Again they heard him grind and sing for a few minutes, then he left the house. The watchers jumped up and wanted to grab him, but he jumped over them and tore away from them. The small plaza was filled with people, but he jumped over them and escaped, as he was very strong. But descending the trail to the water he came upon the lonely watcher there, who jumped up, grabbed him, and held him, crying out to the people on the plaza: "I have the dualangwu." So the people rushed down to the water and saw that the young man had caught the ghost. The people then led him back to the village and put him into a kiva, made a light, and there they saw a Yahponcha sitting. The father had told him that in the fourth night they would capture him, and so this became true.

Hereupon the crier cried out in the village: "You that are living here, all of you come and assemble here." So the people all assembled there and filled the kiva. The old men were crying and said: "There is some reason for this, certainly it is not without some purpose that he goes around this way and acts so. He certainly wants to do something bad." The village chief now requested that some one go and take off the masks from the ghost. Then some one approached him, but the masks were fastened securely around his neck, so the man cut the strings with his knife and took off the first mask and laid it on the floor, and behold! There was another mask. So he took that off and laid it on the floor, but found that there was another mask, and he took that one off and laid it on the floor. But he saw that there was a fourth mask and that was a Katcin-mana mask, so he took that off and they all looked at the personage, and behold! It was the chief's son. "Puyaami!" they all said (an expression of regret and sorrow). "That is the chief's son!" They found that he had some bahos tied to each wrist and to each ankle. These they untied, also placing them on the floor.

He was a nice, clean, handsome youth; had turquoise ear pendants, and many nice beads; his head was nicely washed, and on his face he had two black lines painted with yalahai, two lines running from the upper part of the nose to the cheeks. The young man who had now been exposed then said: "Take these bahos and thrust them into the ground, one at the plaza, and the others in the different corners of a house," which he designated. He furthermore told them that for four days they should have a feast, and having said this he left the kiva and went to his home. The people thought about it a great deal and were unhappy. They did not know what it meant, and whether or not some evil was planned for them, but they killed their sheep and prepared a feast and ate and feasted for four days. During the third day, they especially prepared much food, and were feasting all day and all night; still many of them were looking for and expecting some evil to befall them the next day, but the sun rose higher and higher and nothing happened to them, and when evening came they felt very much relieved, saying: "Nothing has happened to us," and they became happy again. Thus three years passed without any especial evil happenings, but in the fourth year something happened. The young man when telling the people that they should feast for four days, had not told them right.

The people had been right in their suspicions that something evil might befall them after their four days of feasting, but instead of it happening after the four days, the plan of the ghost had been that it should happen at the end of four years, which, however, he had not told them. In the fourth year the expected evil came upon them. The old man, who had four years before complained to the village chief of the bad conduct of the young men of the village, was still living. He was still angry, and in the fourth year he prepared many bahos of hard wood: tuvavi, mopuovi, tave, kwingvi. He made the points of the bahos very sharp and made very many of them. In the fall of the fourth year when they had gathered in their crop, the village chief said to the crier chief, who was also bad and in league with the village chief: "Our time has now come. You cry out that the people again should feast four days." So the Crier Chief announced saying: "You that live here, thus I am informing you, all that have something living, kill the same and eat it for four days. All that have something good, eat it and have a feast." But the people were full of mistrust. They were afraid that at the expiration of the four days some evil would befall them, and they did not comply with the requests of the chiefs; they did not prepare a feast.

During the night following the announcement the chiefs met with the aforesaid old man, who told them that they should dress him up and put him into the tiwonyapavi (Katcina shrine on the plaza in which there was a stone image of a Katcina and which was supposed to belong to the Katcinas). So they dressed him up, painting his back black, his chest and abdomen red, and both sides of the front part of his body green. On the arms, chest, and legs they made the typical marks of Po'okong (two short lines). To the back of his head they fastened a pohtakni, of the tail of a sparrow-hawk, extending upwards with the points of the feathers. To the top of his head they fastened a horn. His face was also painted black. He was to represent the Balolookong. He wore no costume.

When they were done they went to the plaza during the night when all the people were asleep. They dug a hole in the shrine already mentioned above, so that it would admit the man entirely. Hereupon they placed in his arms all the bahos that he had made, and with them they placed a Balolookong whistle. They also gave him a little bowl with some water, into which he could blow the whistle, as is still done in some ceremonies. They then covered up the opening with a large flagstone, covering earth and dust over it to destroy all appearances of the opening that had been made, and finally placed a piece of native cloth over it. They then commenced to sing some sorcerer's songs. When they sang the third song, the old man in the ground began to eject rumbling, roaring sounds, and told the chiefs: "I have been successful, I have reached my object." "All right," they said, and left the old man remaining in the ground. None of the inhabitants of the village had noticed anything. The buried man then thrust about half of his hand through an opening that he had made, and when the people arose in the morning, they noticed the hand and said: "Something is protruding here." The old man then sang:

Ala kwikwi, ala kwikwi,
Ala kwikwi, ala kwikwi, kwi--(with a rising inflection).

As he sang the last word he lowered his little finger. The sun was now rising. The next morning he sang the same words, lowering the next finger, and on the third morning he again sang the same song and lowered the third finger. By this time the people, who had seen and heard it, felt very unhappy and were afraid that some evil would befall them. They now noticed, that at the places where four years previously the bahos had been planted by the direction of the ghost, water began to come out of the ground. These bahos had really been Balolookongs, who, it seems, had finally entered the ground and were now bringing out the water from the ground.

The people now became alarmed and began to suspect that probably a flood was about to destroy their village. That night they killed their sheep and prepared food and had a great feast, thinking that probably the next day they would all be destroyed anyway. On the fourth day just before sunrise, the old man in his grave sang the same words again and lowered the fourth finger as he finished his little song. Immediately he emerged from the opening in the form of a large Balolookong, and now Balolookongs were shooting forth from the ground with streams of water in all parts of the village, from the fireplaces in the kivas, in the houses from the water vessels, and in fact everywhere. Water began to fill the houses in the village. Soon the houses began to fall, burying many of the inhabitants under the falling walls. A number of them fled to the higher places on the east side of the village, where there was a large, strong house. In one of the houses a few old men climbed up on the shelves on which are usually placed the trays with corn meal in Hopi houses. Here they sat in a crouched position and turned into turkeys. The water rose so high that their tails began to hang into the water. It did not reach the houses in the eastern part of the village where the people had assembled. None of the chiefs were destroyed. So when they had assembled in the house mentioned the chiefs met in council and asked what they were going to do now. So they began to make bahos, took beads and turquoise, first crushed them and then ground them into powder. Of this powder they made two balls which they placed onto a tray on which they also had placed the bahos that they had made. There were a great many of these bahos. They then called the Village Chief's son, who had caused the destruction, and his sister, a very pretty maiden. They dressed up the latter in the same manner in which the Flute-manas are costumed, putting a white robe on her, over which they tied a white kilt, and an eagle-breath feather in her hair above her forehead, beads around her neck, etc. Her chin was painted black, white lines running from ear to ear over her upper lip.

The young man was clothed in a plain white kilt and black zigzag lines were painted on his legs, arms, and the back and front part of his body. These two were to drive back the Balolookongs. The water was still coming out of the ground and the Balolookongs still shooting swiftly through the water. The one that had been the old man, who was buried on the plaza, was the largest and most powerful of the Balolookongs and was still standing at the place where he had emerged from the ground. The rumbling of the falling houses could still be heard. When the two were dressed, the young man took some bahos in his left hand, the mana took the tray containing the two balls and the rest of the bahos, and thus they began to wade into the waters. They made straight for the large Balolookong, which was considered the chief of the water serpents. Arriving at the place where he stood, the young man grasped and encircled the serpent with both arms and pressed him down into the water, whereupon the serpents as well as the young man and his sister disappeared under the water and never returned.

Immediately the water began to fall and disappear in a comparatively short time, the powder of the beads and of the turquoise, which the mana had brought to the water serpent as an offering, causing the ground to dry and to become hard quickly because the powder was made of very hard substances. The water-serpents had all disappeared, but so had the young man and his sister. The place where the village had stood was full of mud and the people could not get there for some time yet. Everything was destroyed there. Only the old men who had been turned into turkeys survived. They had been very old and bald-headed, which is the reason that the turkeys to-day have no hair or feathers on their head. In one house, however, which stood somewhat high, two children, two little brothers, had been sleeping during the flood and had not been drowned, but they had very little to eat now. The younger one had found a little piki in a tray, which they ate.

The people in the eastern part of the village soon set to work to prepare to emigrate. They baked piki and made other food of the provisions that they still had left. Early in the morning the day after the water serpents had disappeared they took some of the food which they had prepared, and made a food altar (tono'sh-pongya), eastward from the village. Packing up the things, and especially the food which they had prepared, they all passed by this food altar, the village chief at the head of the line. Each one took a little quantity of each kind of food that they had placed there and ate it. They then passed on. The ground was still soft and muddy from the flood. The two children that had survived in the village had not been found and were left. They soon became hungry and hunted something to eat. Occasionally they would find a little corn hanging on some of the walls that were still standing, or some other food the older brother would carry his little brother on his back. In the evening they would cry because they were lonely. The turkeys that had been Hopi saw the children and pitied them, but, although they cried over them so that the tears would roll from their eyes, they could not say anything to them. Finally one of the turkeys took such a pity on the children that he commenced to talk to them. "You poor ones," he said to them, "how will you take care of yourselves here? There is some corn hanging on the walls yet, but you cannot reach it. You go to the east there to those other houses. There the people made food when they left. There is a food altar standing there yet, of which you may eat!" So the children went there and found many trays full of piki standing on the ground. Of that they satisfied their hunger. They also found a few rabbit-skin blankets in a house and so they lived there.

The people that had left the village traveled on. One day the big Balolookong came out of the ground again and looked after the people. The place where he came out was now a large opening like a koici (a cistern-like oven in which sweet corn is steamed). He was a very large serpent and (the Hopis say), as no one was there to put him back again, he remained standing there. The two children by and by consumed all the food that they had found there and they began to suffer. They wanted to go back to their house but saw that water serpent standing there, and so they were afraid and did not know how to get back to their house, but their food was nearly all gone. Balolookong saw the children and had sympathy with them. They were the children of his daughter so he was their grandfather. He cried over their fate, the tears rolling down his cheeks. Stretching up high, he looked whether the mother of the children had gone very far, and saw the people, as they had not moved away very far, but the children were still afraid to go back to their house. Finally the serpent began to speak to them in Hopi: "Come here. Come here. Be not afraid of me, I am your grandfather." The children looked up and listened when they heard somebody speak to them. So they went to the serpent, who said to them: "I am your grandfather. I pity you, but what will you eat here? There is some corn yet, but you cannot reach it, it is hanging so high on the walls. You find a place where there is some sweet corn strung on a string hanging on the wall; then pile up some stones, and climbing on the stones, throw some of the ears down with a stick. These you take with you as food and then follow your parents. They are not very far yet and you will overtake them. But whenever you get ready to go you come here to me first. Now you go and hunt a knife, and if you find one bring it to me, maybe I shall want to follow them sometime, too." So the children went through the houses and sure enough found a sharp knife of flint. They also found in one of the houses some corn hanging on strings on the wall not very high up. They piled up some stones and loosened some of the corn-ears with a stick so that a good deal of it fell down. This they ate and satisfied their hunger. They intended to leave the next morning. "To-morrow we will follow our parents," they said. So the next morning early they went to their grandfather and said to him that they would now go. He asked them whether they had any food to take with them. They said: "Yes, we have wrapped up some of the corn that we have found strung up and hanging on some of the walls and that we have thrown down." He said: "You follow your parents, and I shall stand here and keep looking after you so that nothing will happen to you. But you take your knife and be not afraid, but cut a piece out of my back. This you take with you and give it to the chiefs and tell them: "This is a piece of meat from the Balolookong, and when at any time it does not rain you make bahos and rub a little of this meat among the paint with which you paint the bahos, and it will certainly rain." The children refused to cut out the piece of flesh, saying: "That will hurt you very much." "No, no," he said, "be not afraid." Finally they were willing, took the knife and cut out quite a large piece of flesh. They found that the meat was very tender and when they had cut out the piece the wound closed up immediately.

So they started after their people. In the evening they were very tired and slept all night. The next evening they were again very tired and slept on a ridge that was covered with pine-trees. The older brother carried his younger brother and also the food and he was nearly exhausted. They were also very thirsty and hungry, but they were so weak that they could hardly eat the hard corn. On the third day at about noon they were nearly exhausted and were very thirsty. They sat down under a pine-tree. Their food was also all consumed. As soon as they had sat down they fell over and fell asleep.

Cotukvnangi, the God of Thunder, lived in the sky and saw the children and took pity on them. He concluded to descend and help them. He took a gourd vessel full of water and some rolls of nuva-muhpi (piki made of meal of fresh roasting ears) and then descended to where the children were. They were sleeping, their mouths where dry and parched. Soon the younger brother awoke and there somebody was sitting by their side, somebody very terrible. The personage had three very long horns or projections on the head, two standing sideways, and one standing upward on top of the head. They were of ice. His costume also consisted of ice and was full of little fringes or icicles that rattled all over his body. On the head he also had two large ice ridges representing clouds.

The little boy was very much frightened and grasped his brother and cried: "Get up, there is somebody here." So the elder brother jumped up and beheld the Cotukvnangi. He also was very much frightened and the two children embraced each other and cried. While the children looked downward, Cotukvnangi removed his mask and when they again looked up they saw a very handsome man. "Do not cry, do not cry," he said to the children, "here, drink; I have brought some water for you," and handed them the gourd vessel, from which they drank and quenched their thirst. He then handed them the food, and they ate it and satisfied their hunger.

You remain here, "he said," you remain here at least two or three days and eat and drink this, and when you have recovered and become strong then follow your people. They are not far away. They are right east of here." After he had said this and the children were not just looking towards him he rose again and disappeared in the sky. When the children looked for him he was gone.

So they slept there that night, staved the next day and remained another night, and the following day at about noon Cotukvnangi again appeared to them bringing them some more of the same kind of food, also some water melons and drinking water. Cotukvnangi remained with them that afternoon and after the sun had gone down he began to talk to them, talking to them all that night. Cotukvnangi is the great warrior chief, and he now gave to these two youths the lightning and the thunder, and he told them how to kill enemies and that when they had killed their enemies they should take their scalps; and he taught them the songs that they were to sing when they returned from their war expeditions and after they had killed some one, and told them that when they came to their home they should throw the scalps into the kiva, on the cloud symbol made with corn-meal by the warrior chief. They should then cut out a round piece of bear skin which they should place on the floor in the kiva and encircle it by a line of corn-meal. The warrior who had brought home the scalp should sit on this bear skin for three days and three nights, and on the morning of the fourth day the warrior should wash his head in the kiva (tokasnaya). Then he should go to his home where his k'aamu, should also wash his head. Then he should put the scalp which he had brought on a stick and perform a dance on the plaza in which his kaamu should accompany him.

After having thus explained to them many things about wars, and taught them many war and battle songs all night, it had become morning and he told them that now they should follow their people, He told them that their parents would probably not know them, but they would ask who they were, and they should then take hold of their mother and tell her who they were and she would then probably know them. Then Cotukvnangi returned to the sky. The lightning arrow (hohu) and the thunder he had promised them, but had not yet delivered to them. He told them that whenever they needed them, wanting to go and kill some one, they should pray to him and he would give them those things. So the two brothers started off after they had refreshed themselves with the morning meal once more. Arriving at Homolovi they came upon their people. They lived in two little villages, and in the one farthest north only a few people lived, and here they found their mother.

The older brother was still carrying his younger brother as the latter was very tired. "Somebody has come," the people said. "Who has come? Whose children have come? Where are you from?" they asked. "We are from way over therefrom the village," they said. "We have followed you. You have gone this way and our mother and our father are here and we have come after them." So they called the people together and said: "Come here and see if there is anybody here who did not bring their children with them," and then the people gathered around the children. The people commenced to ask now the different women whether there was any one who had failed to bring their children with them, but no one was found. They also asked the mother of the two children but she also denied. When no one could be found that would claim the two boys, they recognized their mother and went to her, taking hold of her hands, and said: "Our mother, we have come," then the mother remembered and acknowledged that her two children had remained in the house sleeping when they had fled, but she, of course, had thought that they had perished. And when she now saw her children before her, she embraced them and cried. So the children remained with their mother.

The people living in the smaller village were the Batki-namu. Those living in the larger village were the people most of whom later constituted the Forehead clan (Kal-namu). The two youths the told the people about the piece of flesh that they had cut from the back of Balolookong, and had brought with them. So when the Batki people made bahos they rubbed a little of this meat into the paint with which they painted the bahos, and then it thundered and rained. Before that it had rained only a very little, and hardly ever was there any lightning and thunder. After this there came heavy rains and weather, which made the Batki people "Great Batki" people'

The two youths grew up to be young men, but they became bad, warring and fighting the Hopi children and the other youths, and when they had grown up they remembered what their father, the Thunder, had told them. They said to each other: "We have now grown up, let us go out and ask our father for what he has promised us, and then let us go and kill some one." To their mother and the people they said that they were going to kill some deer, and so she prepared some food for them and they started off. In the evening they gathered some wood and built a fire. Cotukvnangi saw them and came down to them again. "You have now reached your object," he said to them. "Yes," they replied. "It is well that you have come," he said. "Close by here are some Apache, and whoever becomes a warrior for having killed them, he is a great warrior, because they are fierce. These Navaho do not amount to much, and it is well that you have come in this direction." So during the night he instructed them bow to go out and kill the Apache, also teaching them some war songs. Hereupon he went home again. He first told them, however, that he would watch them, and that he would kill their enemies for them. They would do it, he said, but it would be he that would do it through them. Then when they were through they should come back again and he would come down again, then they would talk together and from here they should go back again to their home.

So in the morning they proceeded and soon came upon some Apache (Utsaamu). There were a great many of them, who at once became-excited and ran towards them and began to surround them. The two brothers at once began to shoot arrows into the crowd for some time, but did not hit any one, neither did the Apache hit them. The brothers had put the lightning (talwipiki) and the thunder (umu'kpi) under their clothing. After they had been shooting for some time, they became tired, and the older brother all at once said: "Now then it seems they are upon us. How long yet will this last? Hereupon he drew forth the lightning and the thunder and aimed at the Apache and shot the lightning into the crowd. All their enemies were slain, their camps burned up, and the two brothers laughed at their slain enemies. The Apache had previously made many raids on the Hopi at Homolovi, and for this reason the two brothers had finally gotten very angry and taken revenge upon their enemies.

Among the Apache warriors had been one very large and fierce one. This one they hunted up among the slain, scalped him and cut out his heart. Then taking the moccasins and costumes from all the slain, they returned, While they had killed all the warriors they had destroyed only one tent in which there had been women and children. This had been blown to pieces by the thunder. The objects in the other camps, in which the women and children were, they had left untouched. When they again arrived at the place where they had previously camped, Cotukvnangi again descended and talked with them during the night. He gave them further instructions with regard to warfare, but among other things he told them that they should not be the war chiefs among their people, but when they now came to their village, whomever they should select, on him they should throw the scalp which they had now brought, and he should be the war chief.

In the morning Cotukvnangi again ascended and the two returned to their home, singing war songs as they went along. They went, however, to the larger village, as in the village where their mother lived there were so very few people, and here the rejoicings and rites, to be mentioned presently, occurred. When they arrived at the village they were received by the shouts of their people, who surrounded them, and snatching away the trophies that they had brought with them, swung them around, by which it is said they were discharmed from any bad influence, and then they threw them among the people--a custom which was always observed when Hopi warriors returned from their expeditions.

While the rejoicings and wranglings were going on, the older brother took the scalp which he had been carrying on a stick while they were dancing, and forcibly threw it at one of the inhabitants from the larger village, saying: "It is you, you shall be our war chief. We give this to you. You shall lead us after this." Hereupon they followed him, going around the village four times. They then entered the kiva where the two brothers instructed them as to the rites to be observed in connection with their warfare. They drew the cloud symbol already referred to on the floor, whereupon the newly appointed war chief threw the scalp upon the symbol. They then cut out a piece of bear skin, sprinkled a ring of corn meat around it, and placed the war chief upon it, where he had to remain for three days. Hereupon followed the public war dance on the plaza on the fourth day.

The people lived here in Homolovi a number of years, but how many cannot be ascertained. Finally they concluded to move on north-eastward because, it is claimed, there were so many mosquitos there which would sting their children and their people and caused great suffering. The Hopi say the reason why the people held out so long, although they always suffered from the mosquitos, was that they had such good fields there from which they raised good crops. The mosquitos are called by most of the Hopi salt flies (o'ong-totoptu), but they are also called shipaulavitu by some, from which it seems the present inhabitants of the village of Shupaulavi have derived their name. Then the migrating party had reached a certain bluff, called Coyote Spring Bluff (probably about twenty-five or thirty miles northeast of Winslow), they remained there, but not very long it seems. Here they separated, the Batki clan proceeding northeastward to Aoatovi , the others going northward towards a place a few miles west of Mato'vi. Here they again remained for a number of years as they had good fields there. They finally proceeded farther north to a place called Nashiwamu (about a mile south of Shongopavi), where they probably remained about three years. Just as they arrived at this place, the sun arose, the upper part of the sun (his forehead, the Hopis say), just looming up above the horizon.

For this reason they were ever afterwards the Forehead clan (Kal-namu). They made repeated efforts to get permission from the village chiefs of Shongopavi to move on the mesa into the village, but their efforts were unsuccessful. It seems that the chief had heard something of their doings in Palatkwapi, because he claimed that they were dangerous, bad people (Nu'nukpantu). In the third year they concluded that they would return to their previous home at Homolovi.

The chief of Shupaulavi, which village, however, was not called by that name at that time, but was called Waki (refuge house), heard that these people were going to return and so he went to them and invited them to move up to and settle down in his village, which invitation they accepted, They are still by far the most numerous clan in the village of Shupaulavi. The village was from that time called Shupaulavi, after the name of the new arrivals, who were called by that name because they had fled from Homolovi on account of the mosquitos which they called by that name. At that time Shupaulavi was considerably larger than Shongopavi, the latter having lost a great many inhabitants a long time before, when the people of that village killed a number of Spanish and destroyed their missions, on which occasion a number of Shongopavi fled to Shupaulavi.

The chief of Shongopavi seems to have borne a grudge against Shupaulavi, because later on he informed the Spaniards in New Mexico, probably at Sante Fe, that they should come and take away the inhabitants of Shupaulavi, and said that this was the latter's own wish. So one time the news reached the villages that many Spaniards had arrived at Keams Canyon where they were camping. The next day they came to Walpi where they inquired who it was that wanted to be taken away. The chief of Walpi and the chief of Shupaulavi were good friends with each other, and as soon as the Walpi chief heard about the matter he quickly proceeded to Shupaulavi and informed his friends about it, saying: "The Spaniards have come because they have heard that you wanted them to come and take you east. They have come for you and for no one else," "That is false," the Shupaulavi chief said. "It is not I that want that, it must be some one else. It is probably the chief of Shongopavi." "All right," the chief of Walpi said, "you had then better go and meet the Spanish chief and tell him about it. You take some presents with you, perhaps a tu'ihi and a blue shirt. Give these to this Spanish chief, shake hands with him, embrace him, and tell him how the matter is." So the chief of Shupaulavi wrapped up a tu'ihi and a blue shirt and went with his friend. When they arrived in the kiva where the leader of the Spaniards was, the latter, who was a powerful man, stood and looked at the new arrivals with his arms akimbo. The two men eyed each other for some time. Finally the Spaniard gave the Shupaulavi chief his hand and shook it. The Shupaulavi chief embraced him, the

Spanish officer doing the same. All people present were crying. The chief at once drew forth the presents which he had brought, and handed them to the Spanish officer. "This is yours," he said. "I have heard that you came to get my children and my people. It is not I that wished it, it must be some one else. It certainly is not I." The Walpi chief then asked the officer: "Is this the man that carne to you and said that he wanted you to come and get his people?" "No," the officer said, "this is not the man." "Thanks, thanks, thanks," the Hopi said on all sides, and came and shook hands with the officer. "Thanks that this is not the man."

"No," he repeated, "I never wanted that, it must be the chief of Shongopavi." The officer then said that the next day he would bring his soldiers to a place west of Walpi where there was a large pool of water at that time. He said that they were tired and would rest there awhile. He also explained that they had brought with them a good deal of clothing which they had wanted to give to the people which they had expected to take along. "Now," he said, "What shall we do with these clothes? You tell your people that they should come to-morrow when we are camping there at that water and visit us, and if any of them have anything that they would like to sell we would like to trade with them, giving them clothing which we have brought along, and taking back some of your things."

The Shupaulavi chief consented to this and went home and told his people about it. All were very happy now that thc impending danger had been averted. The next morning after they had eaten their breakfast the people from all the villages proceeded to the camp of the Spaniards where they were trading all day. In the evening the Hopi all returned to their villages, the Spaniards camping there for the night. In the morning after breakfast the latter returned.

After that the Spaniards never encroached on the Hopi any more, but the Shongopavi chief, whose village at that time was very small, spread the news that the Spaniards would come back again some time to Shupaulavi and got them. This so scared the people at Shupaulavi that a majority of them left the village and moved over to Shongopavi, which it is said accounts partly for the small number of inhabitants in the village of Shupaulavi.

How Ball-head (Tatciqto) Wedded and Oraibi Maiden

Told by Macahongva (Oraibi)'

Haliksai! In Oraibi the people were living. At the place where Tuwa-mana now lives, right east of the public plaza, lived a maiden who persistently refused to marry any of the young men of the village, although many of them were wooing her. North of the village at Achamali, lived an old woman with her grandson. "My grandmother," he said to her one time. "What is it?" she answered. "Yes," he said, "I am going to visit that maiden there in the village, and see whether she will not marry me." "Alas!" she replied, "she will not want you," "I am going to try it anyhow," he answered. So one evening, after they had eaten, he put his wildcat robe on, of which at that time nearly every young man had one, and proceeded to the village. It was moonlight.

When he came to the house he stood outside at the corner of the house. The maiden was grinding corn opposite an open window. He went up to the place where she was grinding corn, looked through the opening, and saw that she was very busy grinding corn. "Stop a little," he said. She stopped and asked: "Why do you want me to stop?" "Yes," he said, "I came to you." "Who are you?" she asked. "Yes," he said, "it is I." And hereupon she began to guess, mentioning many names of young men in the village, and asked whether he was that one or that one. Finally she said: "Are you not living north of the village there?" "Yes," he answered. "So you are that one," she said. "All right, I am willing that we should live together." "That is what I came for," the young man said. "Very well," the maiden replied, "I shall ask my mother, and if she is willing, we shall live together. So you go home now and sleep."

After he had left she went down and spoke to her parents, telling them that the young man living north of the village at Achamali had asked her to marry him. They said that they would be glad if he would live with them and he was welcome, "If he has not spoken a falsehood he will certainly come back again," they said. Whereupon they retired for the night.

When the young man arrived at his home, he was asked by his grandmother what he had found out. "Yes," he said, "I have good news; she is willing." Hereupon they too retired for the night. In the morning the grandmother said to her grandson: "You have a big field here. Some of your corn has certainly matured, so you prepare some steamed sweet corn." "Very well," he said. So he gathered some sweet corn-ears, heated his oven, and threw into it a good many corn-ears. In the evening they were done. He took them out, took off the husks, and strung the corn-ears on strings of yucca leaves, preparing about ten bunches of corn ears. By this time the sun had gone down. After a little while he wrapped up the corn-ears that he had strung up, and proceeded to the village.

The maiden was still grinding corn. He left the presents on the ground in front of the house, on the plaza, and went up. "Have you come?" the maiden said. "Yes," he replied. "Very well," she said, come in." Hereupon he went down, got his bundle, and brought it in. A fire was burning at the fireplace. He took a seat by the side of the fireplace. The maiden stopped her grinding and took a seat on the opposite side. The young man had a mask on with three nodules on top, from which small turkey feathers were suspended. It was the Ball-Head (Tatciqto). He handed the maiden the sweet corn-ears that he had brought, saying to her, "You take this and eat it." She was happy and thanked him for it. "Thanks," she said, "on your account I shall eat it." Hereupon she took part of the corn down to her parents who were also glad, and ate of it because they were new corn ears.

Returning to the room where the young man was sitting, they conversed together for a while. "Very well," the maiden said, "I shall now save the corn-meal that I am grinding, then sometime I shall come over to your house." Whereupon they separated, the young man going back to his house, and the mana also retiring for the night. Hereupon the maiden ground blue corn for four days. On the fifth day she ground white corn. Every evening the young man brought over some fresh sweet corn-ears, which the people of the house ate. In the evening of the fifth day he did not bring any, but he came to fetch his bride. She and her mother filled a large tray full of the white meal, tied it up in an ato'o, which she then took in her hands, and followed the young man to his house. When they arrived there he went in first. His grandmother welcomed the maiden to her house and invited her repeatedly to come in. The young man also told her to come in.

So she entered. She first handed the tray with meal to the grandmother, who thanked her for it, and put the meal away. They then ate the evening meal, which consisted of corn, melons, and watermelons. After having conversed for some little time they retired for the night, the mana sleeping with the grandmother. Early in the morning when the yellow dawn was appearing the grandmother and the maiden went out to kuivato (to make prayer-offerings, consisting of sacred meal, to the dawn and rising sun). Returning to the kiva, the grandmother got out four Kohonino trays (chukavotas) and a lot of corn, which the mana was shelling, filling the four trays. When they were filled, the grandmother told her grandson to go and call his animals.

He went out and called them by saying "pi-pi-pi-pi!" whereupon a great many chickens came running to the kiva. When they had come in, the young man first took one tray, scattering the corn to the chickens. When they had eaten that he scattered the corn from another tray, and so on until they were all emptied. He then told them to sit down on the banquette that was running along the wall all around the kiva, which they did. The four empty trays he placed in a row north of the fireplace, Hereupon he said to the chickens: "I am going to sing for you now, so you listen to me attentively, and then afterward s sing the same way."

Hereupon he hung a little drum over his shoulder, gave a signal on the drum, when all the chickens looked at him and listened attentively, while the young man sang the following song, accompanying it by beating the drum:

Aha ihi aha
Kowakoho ngumanta (The chicken was grinding meal),
Angwushihi ngumanta (The crow was grinding meal).
Takahayakwi, tanaymahka.
Ahaha! ihihihihii!

The mana was sitting near the fireplace. While the young man was singing the song, the chickens all swayed their bodies from side to side to the time of the singing, and by doing so ground the corn which they had taken into their bodies. When he had sung the song five times he said to the chickens: "Now then, come and vomit your meal into these trays." So one after the other came and vomited the meal which it had ground in its body into the tray. It was very fine white meal. When they were all through they left the kiva.

In this way the chickens assisted the maiden in getting all that corn ground quickly, so that she did not have to grind it herself as is usually the case. This meal they then used afterwards. But the young man had no cotton, and so no bridal costume was prepared for the bride, for which she was sorry. The young man, however, was a hunter and often brought home rabbits and other game. After the maiden had lived there awhile the grandmother said to her: "Now then, you have been here a long time, you prepare some good food." This the mana did in the morning, preparing some pik'ami and other food. The young man again went hunting and returned with rabbits. The grandmother prepared a great deal of no'qkwiwi. In the evening they spread the food on the floor, filling a great many bowls and trays. When they had spread out the food the grandmother went out and called out: "You my neighbors here, come in and eat, and be not slow about it, but come in and eat."

Hereupon the three sat down and commenced to eat. While they were eating the people began to come in. The first one that came in carried under his arm a large white bridal robe; the second one a small bridal robe; the third one a white knotted belt; the fourth one a pair of bridal moccasins; and the fifth one a reed receptacle. Having placed the same on the floor, they sat down and ate. Hereupon they exhorted the young man, saying to him that when he would now take his bride home and live there in the village he should be good to the people and he should not be angry at them, but should benefit them, whereupon they left the kiva.

Early in the morning the grandmother made some yucca suds and washed the mana's head. When her hair was dry she took her out and sprinkled meal to the rising sun. When they returned, she dressed her up in the bridal costume. The young man put four watermelons in a blanket, and just as the sun was rising they all went out, the grandmother sprinkling a road of meal for her children, and then told them to go on now, whereupon they proceeded to the village, to the house of the bride. Arriving at the house they were welcomed by the mother of the bride who took the bridal costume and also the watermelons, which the young man had brought and put everything away. Hereupon the young people lived in the village, and as the young man was a Katcina the village prospered, it always rained and they had much to eat. But by and by his wife went astray, at which her husband became angry and left the village, returning to his house again. After that it did not rain so much, the people became poor, and it is still that way.

The Aho'li and Other Walpi Katcinas

Told by Kuhkuima (Shupaulavi)

Aliksai! In Walpi and Sitcomovi they were living, but not at the places where the villages now are, but where they used to be. In Walpi lived an old man, the Aho'li Katcina. He had with him a little maiden who was his sister, the Katcin-mana. As he was very old and feeble this maiden would always lead him. In the other village, Sitcomovi, lived a youth with his old grandmother, and as she also was very feeble he took care of her and used to lead her. One time the Aho'li and the little maiden went to their field 'south of Walpi where they wanted to plant. They carried with them little pouches containing seeds. In their field was a baho shrine, and when they came to their field the Katcina first deposited some prayer-offerings in the shrine, first some corn-meal and then also some nakwakwosis which he drew forth from his corn-meal bag. This bag he had tied around his neck.

In this shrine lived Mu'yingwa and his sister Naya'ngap Wuhti. "Have you come?" Mu'yingwa said. "Yes, we have come," they replied. "Thanks," Naya'ngap Wuhti said, "thanks, our father, that you have come. You have remembered us. No one has thought about us for a long time and brought some offering here, but you have thought about us." And she began to cry. Hereupon Aho'li gave to each one a stick upon which some nakwakwosis were strung, and also some corn-meal. Hereupon Naya'ngap

Wuhti was crying still more. "Yes, we have come here," the Katcina said, "we are pitying our people because they have not had any crops for a long time, and now we thought about you here and have brought these prayer-offerings here. And now you pity them and let it rain now, and when it rains then a crop will grow again and they will have something to eat, and they will then be strengthened and revived, because they are only living a very little now.

Hereupon he took out his little bundles of seed and gave to the goddess a small quantity of yellow, blue, red, and white corn as an offering. These he placed before her on the ground. The two deities then arose. Mu'yingwa had in his left hand a mongkoho, mongwikuru, and a perfect corn-ear (chochmingwuu). These he pointed upwards towards the sky. The female deity held in her hand a squash, which was filled with all kinds of seeds, and as Mu'yingwa pointed up the objects towards the sky she raised the squash with both hands, and then forcibly threw it on the ground on the seeds which the Aho'li had placed there. "There," she said, "in this way I have now planted for all of your people these seeds and they will now have crops." Thereupon Mu'yingwa handed the objects which he held in his hand to the Katcina, saying, "You take these with you and with them you produce rain and crops for your children, the people in Walpi."

So the Aho'li and the Katcin-maha returned, first going to their booth, or shelter (kisi), that was near by in the field. Here they partook of the food which they had brought with them. "Thanks," the Aho'li said, "thanks that our father was willing. We shall not now go back to the village in vain." "Yes, thanks," the mana also said. Hereupon they returned to the village. It was now late in the afternoon. As they passed the top of the mesa upon which Walpi is now situated, they heard somebody singing on top of the bluff, but they went on, and arriving at their kiva they sat down north of the fireplace and smoked over the objects which they had brought with them. "Thanks that we have returned," The Aho'li said, "that we have not been too late for our people. We shall now possess our people." And as they were smoking and thus talking somebody came and entered the house. It was the youth who lived with his old grandmother in Sitcomovi. He came in. "Thanks that you have come," he said, "thanks that you have come and provided something for our people here," whereupon he shook hands with them. "Sit down," Aho'li said, "and smoke, too." So the youth filled the pipe with tobacco that he had brought with him and also smoked over the objects. He took special pains to blow the smoke in ringlets upon the objects. After he had done that four times, also praying to the objects, they became moist so that the water was beginning to flow from them, indicating that their efforts had been successful and that these objects would produce rain, which was symbolized by this moisture.

Hereupon the youth prepared to return to his home, but Aho'li restrained him and said: "Now, tomorrow when the sun rises we shall make a prayer-offering and you must do the same, because when we came we heard somebody sing away up there somewhere." So early the next morning they dressed up in their costumes, the Katcina being dressed in a tu'ihi, a kilt, and his mask; his body also being painted nicely. In his right band he carried a stick, nato'ngpi, to the middle of which were tied beads and a bundle of bahos. In his left hand he carried the objects which he had obtained the previous day. The mana was dressed as the Katcin-manas are yet dressed to-day. She carried in her left arm a tray (pota), containing different kinds of seeds. They proceeded to a baho shrine west of the present village of Walpi, half-way down the mesa. Here they sprinkled a little meal to the sun and on the shrine, this little rite being called kuivato. As they were performing this rite they again heard the same voice singing on top of the mesa, which they had heard before.

There were then no villages on top of the mesa, but the shrine of Talawhtoika was there already, and at this shrine some one was singing. When looking up they say that it was the Big-Horn (Wopakal) Katcina. Hereupon they returned to their house, but immediately started up on the mesa to look for and meet the one that they had heard singing. So they went up and reached the top of the mesa somewhat west of the bahoki. Here they noticed some one dressed in a white mask with very small openings for the mouth and eyes. His body was also white and he wore a thin bandoleer with blue yarn over his shoulder. He was standing by the side of the shrine shaking a rattle of bones slowly up and down. After having shaken the rattle four times he started off. "Wait," the Aho'li Katcina said, "wait, we have heard some singing up here and want to see who it is." "Yes," the other Katcina, which was the A'ototo, replied, "yes, I am not singing, but we are two of us here, and the other one was singing." By this time the Big-Horn Katcina came from the west end of the mesa holding in his left hand a bow, and having a quiver strung over his right shoulder. He had a green mask with a big horn on the right side and an ear on the left. He wore a nice kilt, nice ankle bands, and his body was painted up nicely. When he arrived at the shrine he asked the A'ototo: "Why do you tarry here?" "Yes," the A'ototo replied, "these are detaining me." "Why?" the Big-Horn Katcina asked. "We heard some body singing here," the Aho'li replied, "and we came up here to see who it was, and so it is you. Now, what do you think," he continued, "let us go down all together and then we shall possess the people," and he told the Katcinas about what they had obtained and were going to do. So the two Katcinas were willing and they prepared to go down.

The A'ototo took the lead and was followed by the Aho'li Katcina, and the mana, the Big-Horn Katcina coming last. This way they went down a part of the way at a place west of the present village of Hano. Here they made a baho shrine (bahoki), erecting some stones as a mark between the villages of Hano and Sitcomovi. This shrine is still there. They then went farther down to the present gap north of Hano to the large shrine with the twisted stone which is still there. Here they met somebody coming out of that shrine and then going up and down there. It was somebody dangerous (nukpana), who had large protruding eyes and a big mouth in his mask, and many rattles around his body and along the front part of his legs. His arms were painted white, his body red. Around his shoulders he had a small blanket of rabbit skin. On his feet he had old, torn, black moccasins. In his right hand he had a large knife, in his left hand a crook, to which a number of mosililis were attached. It was the Cooyoko, who used to kill and devour children there. When the Katcinas saw him they said to him: "Do not trouble us, we are going to possess these people here. We are going home now. You can destroy the bad ones, since you are bad anyway, but do not trouble us.

Hereupon they descended and went to their home. When they arrived at the house of the Aho'li, which was a very beautiful house, the Aho'li said: "Now, here we are, and you stay with us. It is not good down here it does not rain, but up there where you are it is better. When it will rain here you can go back, but we want to help the people first. So to-morrow morning we shall go to the fields and plant for the people. "During the night they did not sleep but they were singing all night, on their masks, which they had standing in a row in the north side of the room. When the yellow dawn was appearing before sunrise it commenced to rain, and it rained hard. Towards noon the Katcinas dressed up, putting on their masks, went out, crossed the mesa, came to the fields south of the mesa, and there they beheld large fields of corn, patches filled with melons, watermelons, and squashes. Everything was growing beautifully.

Having looked around a little while they turned around, taking with them a watermelon, an ear of fresh corn, and a melon. It was still raining so that their feet sank deep into the ground.

When they arrived close to the mesa somebody met them. It was Big-Skeleton (Wokomasauwuu), who owns the earth and the fields. He lived about half-way down the mesa near the mesa point. He told the Katcinas that they should go up the mesa and prepare a house there and live there, and from there they should perform their rites. So they went up on top of the mesa and have lived there ever since. Soon after that the Walpi also commenced to move up the mesa and build the new village, where it is at the present time situated.

Pookonghoya and His Brother as Thieves

Told by Kuhkuima
(Shupaulavi)

Aliksai! At Shongopavi they were living; at the place where Shongopavi used to be and where there are still the ruins of the old village, they were living. North of the village, but close by, lived Po'okong and his brother. They lived there with their grandmother. Often they would play with their ball, and one time they were also playing with their ball, striking it, and playing with it towards Toriva. When they arrived here they were thirsty, and went into the spring to drink water. When they had satisfied their thirst they were going to continue their playing, when they saw a lot of bahos at the place where the water comes out. "Let us take these along," the younger brother said, and taking one of the bahos, he swallowed it. "You swallow one too," he then said to his elder brother; but by this time the latter discovered in the recess in the rocks somewhat high up, some potsherds, or bowls, with different kinds of paints which the Flute priests had deposited there. "Let us take some of this," he said to his younger brother, whereupon he put into his ball, through little holes and openings that had been made in the buckskin covering through long usage, some of each kind of paint. After having put the paints into the ball he sewed up the holes. Hereupon he replaced the ball again and then said to his brother: "Now let us go, and before we will get home it will rain if we continue to beat our ball now in this way."

So they started, beating the ball towards the Corn-Ear Bluffs that are still standing at the place where the old village of Mishongnovi used to be. One of the brothers was beating the ball forward and the other one backward, and in this way they proceeded to the village. Before they had reached the village, the people of Mishongnovi had discovered them. They were beating their ball around north of the village for a little While, the children of the village looking on and shouting at them. Hereupon they entered the village and kept beating their ball through the village. All at once they entered one of the kivas and found that the Flute priests were assembled in this kiva for their ceremony. In one of the trays that were standing on the floor was lying a lightning frame, thunder board, netted water jug, etc. This tray they grabbed and went out. None of the priests said anything.

Hereupon they went into another kiva where the Snake priests were assembled for their ceremony. They were just washing the snakes in a bowl. The Pookonghoyas grabbed a bull-snake (lolo'okong), put it into a snake-sack and left the kiva, the younger brother holding this bag under one arm, the elder brother carrying the tray with the objects. In this manner they proceeded towards the Corn-Ear bluffs, constantly beating their ball. When they arrived at the Corn-Ear Bluffs they found a great many bahos, little artificial melons, watermelons, and peaches which the Hopi had made and deposited in the different niches, cracks, etc. They had been deposited here by the different societies in their different ceremonies as prayer-offerings, that they might have an abundance of these things. On top of the rocks they saw the Watcher (Tu'walahka), who owns this rock. It was Cotukvnangwuu, who was sitting there in the form of an old man. "Oh my!" the younger brother said, "How many prayer-offerings there are here! Let us steal some of them and take them home;" but the elder brother refused to do so, so the younger brother ascended the rock along a crack and took from one of the places where the prayer-offerings had been deposited a corn baho, a watermelon, and a melon, and brought them down.

Hereupon they started homeward again, beating their ball. They again went by the spring Toriva where they drank, this time, however, not stealing anything. They then started towards Shongopavi along the trail. After they had gone a little distance they shot the lightning frame, and twirled the bullroarer several times. By the time they had reached the canyon, or gulch, right east of Shongopavi, and as they were beginning to ascend to the village, clouds had gathered in the sky and it began to thunder and rays of lightning began shooting through the sky. Soon it began to rain.

They began to run towards their house, and just as they arrived there they once more shot the lightning frame and twirled the thunder board. By this time it thundered very hard and loud, and lightning was flashing. One of the Hopi houses in the village was struck and shattered. By this time they had arrived at their house. "Who are those little mischief makers that are coming there?" their grand Mother said. "You are bad." But the two brothers rushed into the house and put the lightning frame, thunder board, the snake, the little artificial melons, bahos and the paint, which they had brought with them, quickly but secretly into two pots which they covered up. And because the Pookonghoyas afterwards had these things they were the cause that it always rained and the Hopi had good crops.

How Po'okong Won a Bride

Told by Tangakhoyoma (Oraibi)

Haliksai! In Oraibi they were living. There were a great many people. At Pik'achvi lived a family who had a pretty maiden who persistently refused all offers of marriage. Pookonghoya and his brother Balo'onghoya, who lived at Pookongwawarzhpi with their grandmother, Spider Woman, heard about this. They were thinking about it, and one time said to their grandmother: "Our grandmother!" "What is it?" she replied. "There is a maiden in the village," they said, "who refuses to marry any one of the young men of the village. We are going to try, too." "You poor ones," she said, "you are too small and you are unsightly, she certainly will not want you." But they would not listen and said, "But we are going to try it, anyway." "Very well," she said, "you go and try it, but she will not want you because you are not handsome."

So in the evening they took some squash seed and gathered some little sticks and went to the village. West of the house where the maiden lived a great many mice were living among the rocks. Here the Po'okongs set a number of stone traps, putting the squash seed into them. While they were engaged in setting the traps towards evening, the maiden happened to go by there and- saw them at work. "What are you doing here?" she asked. "Yes," they said," we are setting traps here for the mice." "You come to my house and set traps there, too," she said to them; "there are a great many mice there.

So she took them over to her house where they set traps in different parts of the house, also close to the mealing bin. They finally asked whether they did not have a piki tray. The mother fetched one from another room and they set that near the mealing tray, instead of a small stone like in the other traps. "Now, to-morrow you must look after these traps," they said to the maiden, and left. They at once went hunting and killed an antelope. This they took to the house of the maiden during the night and placed it under the piki tray, making it appear as if it had been caught in that trap. When the maiden examined the traps the next morning she found something large under the piki tray, and looking at it she saw that it was an antelope. She at once called her father. "My father," she said, "you go in there. Something large has been caught there, and do not be slow about it." He was still sleeping, but got up at once, went into the room, and saw that something large had been caught there. "Thanks," he said. "Why this is an antelope; why, an antelope has been caught here." Hereupon he took it out of the trap and carried it into his kiva.

Here he skinned the antelope and cut it up into pieces. A part of the meat his wife cooked as no'ekwiwi, the rest he dried, and they were very happy over it. In the evening the Po'okongs took some more squash seed and again repaired to the village, where they set traps as they had done on the previous evening. While they were doing so the maiden was eating of the antelope meat and then again went to the place where the Po'okongs were setting the traps. Here she met them. "Have you come again?" she asked them." Yes, "they replied." When you are done here," she continued, "you come to our house again and set traps there, because something large was trapped there this morning and we are very happy over it."

They went with her to the house and there set traps everywhere again. When they came to the tray the maiden said to them: "Here something large was caught last night and of that we are eating now. We are very happy over it. So you must set that again, too." While they were setting this the father came in and asked them: "Are you setting traps here again?" "Yes," they replied. "Very well," he said, "last night an antelope was caught in this trap and of that we have been eating and we are very happy over it. You have by that terminated something here (referring to the persistent refusals of the maiden to enter into marriage), so if to-morrow morning something is caught in this trap again, you come here to-morrow evening and get our daughter."

In the night the Po'okongs killed a deer, of which they owned many, and carried it to the house of the maiden, where they placed it under the piki tray trap. In the morning when the maiden arose she saw something under the trap with big antlers. Running to her father she called him, saying: "My father, come quickly. There is something large in the trap." So he came and found a deer there. "Thanks," he said, "this is a deer," and taking it out they carried it to the kiva where he skinned it and cut up the meat. His wife again cooked a part of it, while he hung all the rest up to dry. There was a great deal of meat hanging outside of his house and they were very happy over it.

"To-night you wait for somebody here," he said to his daughter. Towards evening they were eating of the meat that the mother had cooked, and in the evening the maiden was grinding corn. In the house of the two Po'okongs the two brothers were getting ready to go to the house of the maiden, but they began to quarrel about it. "I am going," Po'okong said. "No, indeed," his brother replied, "I'm going," and thus they were contending with each other. "Now, why do you quarrel about this?" their grandmother asked them. "Certainly Po'okong must go because he is the older one." Thus she spoke to them.

So in the evening Po'okong proceeded to the house of the maiden, whom he found grinding corn in an upper room. He entered and said: "I have come because your father wished it that way." "Very well," she said, and went to call her father. Her father went to Po'okong and told him; "Yes, you know I told you that you could come and fetch our daughter because you have trapped this game for us, which we are eating and for which we are glad." Hereupon the mother filled a tray with meal for her daughter, and Po'okong then led her away to his house in order to marry her. When they arrived there the grandmother told them to come in, but she doubted whether her grandchild had brought the maiden until she saw her enter. She was then very happy and told them to sit down. She took the tray of meal from the maiden and put it away into an inner room towards the north. Coming out she placed before the maiden a small tray with a very small quantity of hurushuki, and invited the maiden to eat. The latter took the entire quantity and placed it into her mouth. Spider Woman was watching her and when she saw that she put all the hurushuki into her mouth, she said: "You must not do that, why that is 'very something,' and you must just, take a very little of it." So the maiden replaced the hurushuki into the tray and then put a very small quantity into her mouth. When she began to eat this it increased in her mouth so that her mouth was filled. She repeated this until she was satisfied and then there was some of the hurushuki left.

When the maiden had eater they soon retired for the night, the maiden sleeping with the grandmother. Early the next morning the grandmother and the maiden went out to throw an offering of sacred meal to the sun, which they did close by the entrance of the kiva. Returning to the kiva the grandmother, or Spider Woman, got some corn-ears, shelled them, and then the maiden ground this corn for three days. Early on the fourth day when the yellow dawn was rising, the grandmother went out and called out to her neighbors that they should come in and assist in washing the heads of the two. She then went in and brought out the maiden and told her to be sitting close to the kiva entrance and then wait. Soon a great many clouds came and rained upon the maiden, thus washing and bathing her. "Thanks," the grandmother said, "that you have thus washed the bride." Hereupon she took her into the kiva.

The maiden then again ground corn all day, and in the evening prepared some chukuviki. Spider Woman got some meat from one of the inner rooms, of which they then all ate. The next day this was repeated, and the maiden then made some comiviki, and in this way she prepared food for all of them day after day. But she felt unhappy because no one was carding and spinning cotton and preparing a bridal costume for her, as is always done for a bride. That way they were living there for some time. The two Po'okongs were constantly playing with their ball and stick, also with feathered arrows, but no one was preparing a bridal costume for the bride, about which she was very unhappy. But Spider Woman would often go into an inner room and they would frequently hear her say, "Thanks, thanks," to some one, but the maiden did not know to whom she was talking, but there in that room the spiders were preparing a bridal costume, first carding the cotton, then spinning it, placing it onto a loom and then weaving it.

Finally Spider Woman said one day to the bride: "you prepare some pikami now. Your parents are homesick after you and we shall then send you home." The maiden prepared some pikami, and Spider Woman some no'okwiwi, and in the evening the maiden took out the pikami from the oven, Spider woman dipped out the no'okwiwi, and all ate and then retired for the night. In the morning Spider Woman prepared some yucca suds and with it washed the heads of Po'okong and his bride. She then entered an inner room and brought forth a complete bridal costume, which she handed to the maiden. She then again went into an inner room and brought out a large quantity of meat which she handed to Po'okong. He tied it into a bundle. Hereupon Spider Woman dressed up the bride in the bridal costume, the way it is done to-day, and then sent her on to her mother's house. Po'okong followed her, carrying on his back a large quantity of meat.

Before they started Spider Woman instructed Po'okong that when his wife shall have taken him home now to her house and he should stay there, he should not talk much, but in the evening he should sit on the floor with his arms folded over his knees and he should be looking at his wrist bands (by which she meant that he should simply be, sitting there silently, as the Hopi are usually sitting on their floors and observe silence). While they were going to the village the men who had gotten up early were sitting on their housetops and saw them come. "Here somebody is coming," they said. The two went to the house of the maiden's parents where they were welcomed by the mother, who said, "Thanks that you have come," and received from them what they were carrying.

The mother cooked all the meat which Po'okong had brought, in a vessel, and prepared a feast. After they had eaten they sat and conversed. Po'okong sat on the floor with his arms folded over his knees, but instead of looking at his wrist band, he took it off, and holding it before his eyes he looked through it. The people kept looking at him and said among themselves: "So that is his custom, that is the way he does." After they had all conversed a while they retired for the night. Early in the morning Po'okong went to his house to visit Spider Woman. When he arrived there she asked him whether he had done as she had told him to do about the wrist band. He replied: "When we were through eating and they had taken away and all the things, and the men were conversing, I took off my arm band and held it before my eyes and looked through it." "You are naughty," his grandmother said, "I did not tell you to do that way. If any one becomes a son-in-law he has to sit there quietly with his hands folded over his knees close before his face so that his eyes appear to be, looking at his arm band. You are ka hopi."

Hereupon he returned to the house of his wife again. After s(we time it was planting time and the men began to plant. Po'okong went to Spider Woman and said: "It is planting time and we are going to plant." "Very well," she said, and gave him a small parcel of different kinds of corn to plant. This he took over to the house where he saw his father-in-law ready to go and plant. He had prepared a small sack full of corn, but Po'okong said to him: "Do not take that along, I have brought some planting-corn with me." Hereupon he produced a very small parcel. "That is not enough," his father-in-law said. "Yes, let us take this," Po'okong said, "this is a great deal." "Very well," his father-in-law replied, "we shall take that," whereupon he put away the sack of corn which he had gotten ready.

Hereupon they proceeded to the field of his father-in-law and commenced to plant. Po'okong always put one grain into the hole which he had made with his planting stick, but when the man planted the first hill he put in a great deal, the way the Hopi do to-day. When Po'okong saw it he said: "You must not do that way, but just put in one grain, that is enough." The man immediately replaced the corn into the sack and put in one grain of corn only, after that, and when they were done planting they had not planted all the corn. It had kept increasing. The corn, which they had planted, soon grew up and when it rained it became larger and larger. One time it rained heavily and then much grass also came up.

Po'okong went to visit Spider Woman again. "Have you planted?" she asked him. "Yes," he said. "And when it rained a little," she kept on inquiring, "did the grass come up?" "Yes," he said, "much grass and weeds came up." She then told him that a son-in-law ought to help his father-in-law to hoe his field, so he should return and go and do that. He should take his hoe and form ant hills throughout the field (referring to the small piles of sand and earth that are formed as one is drawing a hoe through the ground; in other words, she meant that he should diligently hoe the field). "Very well," he replied, and returned to the house, where he asked for a hoe. They gave him one and he went to the field. Here, however, he laid it down and at once began to hunt ants. Finding a very large ant hill at the edge of the field he put the ants together with the earth into his blanket and formed small ant hills throughout the field, scattering ants in that way all through the corn-field.

The next morning he again proceeded to his grandmother who asked him: "I told you yesterday to go and hoe the field, what have you done about it? How much did you hoe?" "Yes," he said, "you told me yesterday, so I went to the field, laid down my hoe, and then hunted ant hills along the edge of the field, and when I found a large one I placed it into my little blanket and made little ant hills throughout the field, all day." "Now, that is the way you have done again," she said. "You certainly are a fool. I did not tell you that, I meant that when a man is hoeing and he draws his hoe through the weeds from different sides, the earth and sand is drawn together ill little piles, or hills. These are called ant hills. That is what I told you to do. You are a fool, a fool you are. You go back again, take your hoe, and expose the moist ground by removing the dry surface in cutting off the weeds (wiklolantanangwu)."

He returned to the house, and the next morning when they had their morning meal he asked for a little grease of fat. They hunted some, tied it up, and handed it to him. He took his hoe and fat, and went to the field. Here he laid down his hoe and taking a little of the tallow which he had brought with him, he scattered it all through the corn-field, an act which in the Hopi language is expressed by the same word, wiklolantanangwu. Hereupon he returned to the house without having hoed any at all. Early the next morning he again visited Spider Woman. "Have you come again?" she asked. "Yes," he replied. "Now," she said, "you remember what I told you to do yesterday. Have you done that way this time at least?" "Yes," he said, "when we had eaten yesterday's morning meal I asked my wife's mother for some tallow, which she gave me. I wrapped it up and took it along to the field where I scattered it throughout the field." "You are a fool, you are a fool, you are a great fool. I never told you to do that. I told you to go and hoe the corn, and you know if any man hoes and cuts off the weeds he stirs the dry surface and the moist ground appears a little, and this is what I meant, this is what I told you to do. But you go now, take your hoe and you go and hoe the field."

When he returned to the house he found his father-in-law sitting and meditating, evidently being very sad. He had been to the field several times, and although his son-in-law had always gone to the field he did not find any work done there. The grass was growing, the corn was becoming tired (dry) and wilted, and he was thinking whether his daughter should not send his son-in-law away. While he was thus thinking, Po'okong came to the house. When the latter saw his father-in-law sitting there and evidently being very disappointed, he asked him why he was so sad. "Yes," the man said, "I have been thinking about our field. The grass and weeds are growing and the corn is getting tired. There ought to be some corn ears forming by this time, but it is getting dry." "So that is what you are thinking about," his son -in-law said. "Now, you must not think about that any more. I shall go there to-day and we shall finish hoeing that field to-day." Hereupon the two went to the field.

Spider Woman had in the meanwhile asked the clouds to hoe the field of her grandchild, and when the two commenced to hoe, a cloud was forming over the San Francisco Mountain. Soon many clouds began to move towards the village. When they had hoed a little it commenced to rain. They ran to a shelter where they sat and waited while it was raining. The water soon began to run through the com-field in little streamlets and covered up with sand and earth, the grass in the field. When it stopped raining the two went through the field and saw that the weeds had all been covered up by the floods. "Thanks," the old man said, "that these have cleaned the field for us. We shall go home now." So they went home, and that way were quickly through ridding their field of the weeds.

They were now living happily in their home. By and by Po'okong's wife bore a little son who grew up and played with the children. His father soon made him a bow and arrows with which he learned to shoot. He sometimes shot the Oraibi children and killed them. At this the Oraibi became very angry and said that Po'okong should not live in the village, but they should move away to their own house. So one time Po'okong said, "I am going to go back. I shall take my little son with me, on whose account they are driving us away. But you shall stay here at your father's and mother's," he said to his wife. So he took his little boy on his back and returned to his home where he remained.

How the Antelope Maiden Was Reconciled

Told by Tawiima (Mishongnovi)

Aliksai! At Zuni the people were living, and the two sons of the village chief were racing with each other. At a place called Aamusha some one dangerous (nukpana), lived. A path led by this place, and as the two brothers were racing they came to this bluff and when they were close by they heard some one call, "Come here. There is something beautiful here, come and see it. Oh, no, there is nothing there," the boys said. "Yes, come and see, there is something beautiful here," the voice replied. So they approached closer, and they saw on the top of the bluff a beautiful maiden. It was an Antelope Maiden. She at once drew up the elder brother by a long, deep inhalation. She then said to the younger brother: "Even if you bring your beads here, the most valuable possession of the Zunis, I shall not give you back your brother, as I do not want your beads."

Hereupon the younger brother ran home. "Why do you come alone?" his father said. "Yes," he said, "when we were racing there a beautiful maiden called us and then drew my brother up with her breath, on top of the bluff."Oh!" the father said, "Yes, some one dangerous lives there." The father then told his son to go and hunt up the Pookonghoyas and ask their assistance. He cut a round piece from the middle of a buckskin and made a ball which he tied to a stick; also an arrow, to which he fastened blue-bird and parrot feathers, and finally gave his boy some tobacco and then sent him (on his errand. Going south, he all at once heard some one calling, and saw Pookonghoya and his brother, both being very small, wandering and playing around there. He went first to the house where Spider Woman (So Wuhti), the grandmother of the two brothers lived. She called to the latter and said, "Stop, and come here, some one has come," but they at first did not listen; so she called again. They then came into the kiva and the messenger, handing them the presents, said to them, "This I have brought for you. Way over there lives a pretty maiden who drew my brother up to her, and now my father has made these things and told me to bring them to you in order to see what you thought about it and could do for us." They told him to go westward to the Mole, his uncle. They said he would come to a hollow place where a ladder was protruding, there the Mole lived, and he should see what the Mole thought about it.

So the young man went to the house of the Mole, who told him to go northward to his uncle. So he proceeded northward and came to a little opening in the ground from which there came a breeze. "This must be the place," the young man said, and thereupon a great strong wind came out of the opening. It was the Storm (Hu'k'angwuu), who then invited him to come in, so he went in and found a Hopi sitting in the house. He was a handsome man, nicely dressed up, wearing a bandoleer over each shoulder, also two buckskins tied crosswise over his chest. He wore a hurunkwa on his head, a kilt about his loins, and had black lines on each cheek, while his body was painted up like the bodies of warriors. When they were seated, Hu'k'angwuu asked him why he had come, then he related his story. Hu'k'angwuu then said: "Let us smoke, then we will see what we think about it." So he got out a large pipe and the young man smoked, swallowing all the smoke without again exhaling it. He then said to his host. "Itaha!" "Itiwaya," the uncle replied; and then added: "You are surely my nephew. Now, what is it that you want? What has happened?" He then said: "My older brother and I were racing there and came to a place where a beautiful maiden called us and she drew my brother up, and now my father sent me out to see whether we could do anything to get him back. Our beads, she said, she does not want. His uncle then said, "You go to Walpi (a Hopi village distantly located), and see the Snake people there, who used to have snake dances here and were driven away from here to Walpi when the snakes bit somebody, and see what they have to say about it.

So the young man proceeded to Walpi, although it was far away. So he came to Walpi and there found the Snake people. They were handsome and dressed up like warriors and like Snake people (Tcutcucona).

When he had entered they asked him: "Why have you come here?" "Yes," he said, "we were racing there where we live, and coming to the bluff, Aamusha, somebody spoke to us and said: "You come here, come in here. There is something handsome in here," and then she drew up my elder brother, and now my uncle, Storm, told me to come here and see you. Now, are you the ones, and what now? What do you think about it?" "We shall see," they said, and then began to smoke. The young man again swallowed all the smoke, which pleased the Snakes and they said, "You are truly our nephew. What is it that you want?" "Yes," he said, "we were racing there and that maiden drew up my elder brother and said that she did not want our stone beads even if we would bring them." "Yes," the Snakes said, "she does not want them." The Tcutcucona then showed him a baho, saying, "This the maiden wants, she does not want beads, but she wants such bahos. You look at this baho well and then make one like it; or," they continued, "we shall make one for you. You take that along and then you look at it well and make bahos like it and give them to the maiden. These she wants." So he took one with him and returned home.

When he arrived at his home he showed the baho; they looked at it and then made a good many of them. With these they proceeded to the place where the maiden had enticed the young man. The young man, his father, the two Po'okongs, their grandmother (Spider Woman) and Storm were in the party. Spider Woman had taken a seat behind the ear of Pookonghoya. When they arrived at the bluff the father said, "We have come to get my child." "What have you brought with you?" the maiden replied. "We have brought these bahos," the father said, and hereupon Storm raised them all up and lifted them on the bluff. The mana at once fled into her house, and Storm pushed the whole party into the house also. "What have you brought?" the mana again asked. "This we have brought, this here."

Whereupon they showed her the bahos. "Thanks," she said, "these I want. Of course I shall give him to you, but let us first play a game," whereupon she spread sand upon the floor." Now, you play first," she said. So the Hopi planted different kinds of seed in the sand and thrust the bahos into the sand around the border, whereupon the things planted grew up quickly. "Thanks," she said, "you certainly know something. These I want and you shall certainly take him along. But we shall race first, we shall follow the sun." So she and the young man that had procured the baho arranged for a race. The young man mounted an eagle breath feather, the mana turning into a Tokchii (a swift snake, similar to the racer). They started together, but by and by the mana got ahead of the young man. They circled around the sun, started back, the maiden still being in the lead. Spider

Woman then took a reed, pointed it towards the racers, and by a strong inhalation drew the young man forward, increasing his speed so that he arrived at the house first, thus having beaten the mana in the race. The mana then said, "You take him along, you have beaten me." Whereupon she drew him forth from another room. He was nearly dead. In the inner room were many bones of young men who had perished there. The Antelope Maiden had been angry because no bahos had been made for her for a long time, and hence she had killed so many young men. But since these people now revived her bahos, she was reconciled, and after that killed no more people, and the Zunis were freed from this danger.

How the Yellow Corn-Ear Maiden Became a Bull Snake and Revenged Herself

Told by Qoyawaima (Oraibi)

A long time ago two maidens lived in Oraibi. They were close friends and often used to grind corn together, one time at the house of one, at another time at the house of the other. But after a little while they both fell in love with a certain young man of the village, which led to disagreement and quarrels between them. The Yellow Corn-Ear maiden was possessed of supernatural powers and concluded to destroy her friend and rival. One time early in the morning they were both going to get some water from Spider Spring, which is located somewhat north-east of the village. They took their so-called maiden's jugs (monwikurus) with them. When they were returning to the village they came to a sand hill, and the Yellow Corn-Ear maiden suggested that they rest there for a little while.

After some time she said to her friend: "Let us play here for a little while. You go down this hill and I shall throw something at you. You catch it and throw it back to me," whereupon she drew forth from her bosom a very pretty little wheel that showed all the colors of the rainbow. When her friend had reached the foot of the hill she threw this wheel at her, and when her friend caught it, it was so heavy that it threw her down. When she rose she had been turned into a coyote. Her friend at the top of the hill laughed at her and said, "You have been quarreling with me about that young man, now that is what you get for it. Now, you go about that way." Whereupon she picked up her jug and went to the village.

The other maiden, now a coyote, felt very sad and ascended the hill to her water jug, which she tried to carry but could not do so in her present form. She waited there until evening and was crying most of the time. After dark she tried to enter the village, but the dogs of the village immediately drove her away. She made a large circuit around the village and tried to enter it from another side, but was again driven away by the dogs. So she went westward, and having become very hungry by this time, she was thinking where she might find something to eat. It was in the fall of the year, and the people were watching their crops in the fields, so she thought she might perhaps find something in some of the sheds or temporary shelters in which the people were living, and approaching one of them she found on top of a shelter two roasted ears of corn that had been left there. These she ate. She then made another effort to enter the village but as soon as the dogs of the village smelled her presence she was again driven away. She then concluded that she could not get into the village and again went westward. She knew that somewhere west of Apohnivi there was a place called Yungachaivi, where some herders had also built temporary shelters and were staying while they were herding their sheep at that place. She thought that perhaps there she might find some shelter and food.

By and by she arrived at a hut which belonged to two Qo'oqoqlom Katcinas who were hunting in that region. In this but she found a great deal of rabbit meat, a good many rabbit skins and some entrails of rabbit. The latter and the meat were slightly baked. She was very hungry and ate a little of the entrails, which she did not like very much, however. It was about the time of the morning meal and the two hunters had had their early meat and had already left for the hunt. She was very tired, having spent all the night trying to get into the village and find shelter, and so concluded to remain and rest here all day. In the evening the two Qo'oqoqlom hunters returned. When coming near their hut one of them said, "There is a coyote in our hut and has eaten some of our meat. Let us kill him." Whereupon he got ready his bow and arrows and was aiming at the intruder, when the other one said: "No, let us try to capture him alive and take him home to our grandmother, Spider Woman." Upon entering the hut they heard the coyote sob and saw tears trickling down his eyes. "Oh!" one of the hunters said, "This coyote is sad and has been crying. Let us feed him." So he took a large piece of meat, broke it in two and gave a portion of it to the visitor, who ate it with relish. Hereupon they concluded that they would go home that evening. They tied up the meat and the skins, and also tied the feet of the coyote, and loading everything upon their backs they returned to their home, which was at Katcina Gap (Katcinvala), a short distance northwest of Oraibi.

Arriving there they called to Spider Woman saying, "We have brought you an animal. Come and help us lift it off of our backs." She did so and expressed her satisfaction at the present that she had received. They then placed the coyote and the meat north of the fireplace. The woman looked closely at it and then said to the two hunters: "Alas! that poor one! That is no coyote. Thanks that you have not killed it. Where did you find it?" They told her that they had captured it in their but where they had been hunting, and related all the circumstances. She at once sent one into the village after some Tomoala, the other one she sent to the woods after some juniper branches.

While they were gone she boiled some water, and when the man with the Tomoala returned, she poured the water into a vessel and put a hook from the pods of the Tomoala into the neck and another one into the back of the coyote. She then placed the latter into the water, covered it with a piece of native cloth (mochapu), then placed her hand upon the cover, took hold of the two hooks and kept twisting and turning them, by which operation she pulled off the skin of the coyote. Throwing aside the covering of the vessel she threw away the skin, and in the vessel was found the maiden whom she had thus restored. She still had her clothes on and her hair tied in whorls just as she had left the village. The woman asked her how she had met with this fate, and the maiden told her the whole story. Spider Woman comforted her saying, "You poor one. That Yellow Corn-Ear maiden is bad, but you will take revenge on her."

Hereupon the other hunter returned with the juniper branches. She took the maiden, the branches, and the water into another room and there bathed the maiden, then gave her some corn which the maiden ground into meal. After a number of days Spider Woman told the maiden that she should go home now as her mother was very homesick after her child, but she said she would call somebody in first; so she ascended her housetop and cried out to her neighbors that they should come in. In response to her announcement a great many Katcinas who lived around there came into her house, asking her what she wanted of them. "Yes," she said, "there is this maiden here and I want you to return her to her house," and then told them the whole story. They were willing. She then dressed up the maiden nicely, putting her hair into new whorls and placing over her shoulders a new ato'o, and then instructed her that she should have her father make two bahos and a number of nakwakwosis for the leader of the Katcinas and for the leader of the singing, and also told her how she should behave towards and get even with her enemy, the Yellow Corn-Ear maiden. Hereupon they went to the village, the maiden going in the rear of the line of Katcinas. Having arrived near the house of the village chief (Kik-mongwi), where the Pongowe kiva is at present situated, they performed their first dance, singing while they danced.

This was at early dawn, the so-called white dawn (qoyangwunu). Their singing at once arrested the attention of some of the early risers, who hastened to the place where the Katcinas were dancing. Soon the news was whispered around that the Katcinas had brought a maiden to the village, and some soon recognized the girl and ran to the house of her parents. The latter, however, refused to believe the news, and four messengers had to be sent to them before they believed. They then went to the dancers, who in the meanwhile had arrived at the dancing plaza in the center of the village. "So you have come," the mother said, and began to cry and wanted to take her daughter with her, but the latter said, "Wait a little," and then told her father that he should take two bahos and a number of nakwakwosis, and while he did this the Katcinas continued their dancing and the mana remained waiting by their side. When finally the father brought the prayer-offerings he gave one baho to the leader, the other to his daughter. After the dancing was over, the daughter gave her baho to the leader of the singing. The nakwakwosis were distributed among the other Katcinas, and after the father had thanked the Katcinas for returning his child and had told them that he was very happy, they returned to their home, the parents taking with then] their daughter.

She rested there during the whole day, but early the next morning went to grind corn, singing a little song which told about her recent adventures. Her friend, the Yellow Corn-Ear maiden, heard her sing and at once visited her, expressing her great delight at her return. She was treated cordially, the maiden just having returned not manifesting any ill-feeling towards her at all, according to the instructions of Spider Woman. She was biding her time. They ground corn together all day again as they had done formerly. In the evening they went after water again to the same spring where they had gotten water before. While they were filling their jugs the Yellow Corn-Ear maiden noticed that her friend was dipping her water with a peculiar little vessel (which Spider Woman had given to her) and that the water, as it was running into the jug, looked very beautiful, showing the different colors of the rainbow. She said to her friend: "What have you there? Let me see that little cup." "Yes," her friend said, "that is a very good cup, and the water tastes well from it, too." Hereupon she drank from it and handed it to her friend. She admired it very much and also drank from it. Immediately she fell down and was turned into a bull snake. "There! You remain that way now too," the Blue Corn-Ear maiden said; "you tried to destroy me, but you will now have to remain that way because no one will help you and restore you." She then laughed, picked up her jug and returned to the village.

The bull snake left the place and wandered about. It often gets hungry, but as it cannot run very fast it has difficulty in getting its prey, hence it captures its prey by charming and drawing it towards it by its powerful inhalations, which is still frequently observed by the Hopi. It lives on little rabbits, mice, birds, squirrels, etc., which it charms by its inhalations and then kills them.

This maiden in the form of a bull snake later on went to the village once and there was killed by her own parents, who of course did not know that they had killed their own daughter. Hereupon the maiden, or rather her soul, was liberated and could then go to the Skeleton House. Ever since some of the sorcerers (Popwaktu) will occasionally leave their graves in the form of bull snakes. Bull snakes are often seen coming out of certain graves still wound in the yucca leaves with which the corpse was tied up when laid away. If such a bull snake in which a sorcerer is supposed to have entered happens to be killed, the soul of the sorcerer living in it is set free and then goes to the Skeleton House (Maski).

A Journey to Skeleton House

(Version One)
Told by Qoyawaima (Oraibi)

In Oraibi the people were living, and over there at Honletsnoma's house there lived a youth. He was always sitting at the edge of the mesa early in the morning; He was always thinking about that graveyard there. "Is it true that some one is really living there?" he thought. "Is it true that if some one dies he goes somewhere?" thus he was thinking. "If only some one would tell me whether these that are buried here are living somewhere." Now, at last he got some corn meal, then he went to the edge again, and then he prayed with it to the Sun and said: "Now then, have you perhaps seen anywhere these that are buried here?" Thus he prayed. "Now, if you have seen them somewhere, inform me." Having thus prayed he returned. And then after that he thus continued to pray. After having thus prayed for four days he sat down there and some one came ascending the mesa. The one that ascended asked him: "Now, why do you want me?" "Yes," said the one that was sitting there, "I am always thinking about those who are buried there, whether it is true that they are living in some other life." "Now," he, the Sun, said, yes, they are living. Are you really anxious to see them?" Now the young man answered. "Yes," he said. "Very well," answered the Sun, "I shall then give you this here." He handed him something. "When you will sleep in the evening, eat a little of this, but you tell your mother and them all about it." "Very well," the youth said. "I shall leave," said the Sun.

The young man now went home to his house. He arrived there. His mother was preparing food. When they had eaten he said to his father: "My father," he said, "is it really true that if some one die he remains somewhere? I want to find out about it." Now, hereupon the mother said to him: "You must not do that way; yet it is for you (to say)." "Yes," said the young man, "yes, as soon as I shall sleep in the night I shall not wake up quickly; hence, as soon as the sun is risen and is high up, you must work on me and then maybe I shall return and wake up." Now the father said, "Very well." It now was evening. He now ate a little of the medicine. Upon that he slept. He was entirely dead and he went to the Skeleton House. He came to Apohnivi. There was a plain trail. On the north side he descended and there somebody was sitting, but that one had died long ago and (behold!) it was that one. He recognized him.

That one said, "Have you come?" "Yes," the young man said. "Now you carry me," said the one who was sitting there, "at least four steps. There you set me down." "No, I am in a hurry," the young man said to him, and thereupon proceeded. Now the one that was sitting there cried. When he (the youth) had gone a little was again some one was sitting there. He spoke to him in the same manner. He again did not want to. Now he ascended Bow Height (Aoatovi), but there somebody went backward and forward and carried something. It was a woman. She had in a carrying basket some very hard stone (kalavi), but a bow string was her burden band. It had cut into her head skin. Now that woman said, "Take this from me." "No," the young man said, "I am in a hurry," and proceeded.

.Again somebody came, and now he had reached him, but this one was carrying a mealing stone. His burden band was a hair string. Cactus was tied to the right foot of that one and pona (also a species of cactus) to his left foot, so how could he get along fast? If he hurried a little that pricked him very much. Now that one said, "Take this away from me." "No, he replied, I am in a hurry," and again he proceeded. After that he ran fast. Now then he came to the salt, and there somebody was shaking a bell very loudly. Now he arrived at him, and it was the Kwanitaka. The Kwanitaka said to him: "Have you come?" "Yes," the young man said. The Kwanitaka now said, "Have you seen them? Thus you want it. Now I shall inform you. There where you first came upon one, that one is very wicked. He does not want rain in summer. That one when he does something offensive to these here clouds they all run away. Then again, you know, you arrived at another one. That one killed some one. That one when he put something bad into somebody he died from it, hence when will those arrive here? You see when they have taken four steps, there they remain again. Then these at Aoatovi are carrying something. They also take four steps and then remain there, but they always remain eight 'times' before they proceed, hence when shall they arrive here? Now go on, but you go this way here (pointing to one of two diverging roads). Now you go on happily and then somewhere some one will ring again." And sure enough when he drew near, somebody was ringing, and again he arrived at some one who spoke to him in the same manner. "Have you come?" he said. "Yes," the young man answered. "All right, go on," said the Kwanitaka, and taking hold of the young man he led him. Now they came somewhere, and there was a fire. Now they arrived there and it was very deep there, like a corn steaming oven (koici), but it was burning very much. "Don't you know, those that you first came upon, they come here. Them I burn up here. Those wicked ones there in Oraibi, them I burn up here, but they at least will come out. Do you see, as soon as burned, as soon as it smokes, it comes out? Now you see sometimes it (the air) is filled with smoke. Now that (smoke) is these. They eat nothing. They are never happy. But it was themselves when they planned it. Now then, let us be this way again."

Now they arrived at a place where it was very deep and where it was very dark deep in. "Here I throw some of them in, but they always remain in here. They never come out. Now, come on, let us be back, Thus you wanted to understand this. Now he left him. Now he returned to the other Kwanitaka, and he arrived there. And he again said, "Have you come?" "Yes," said the young man, and again he led him to a road, directing him to the other of the two roads. "That way you go," he said, and now he came somewhere to a village, but it was a large village. They lived there in white houses only. There at the extreme edge of the village a Kwanitaka was going up and down, He said, "Have you come? Come this way," and then took hold of him and took him to the village. He arrived there. There another chief, a Kwanitaka, stood close at the village. "Have you come?" he said to them. "Yes," they answered together, whereupon he said, "Now please enter." Upon that this other also took hold of the young man and they entered, and sure enough, there also some were living and he knew them. He had been a chief in Oraibi a long time ago. Now the Kwanitaka said to the young man. "This way, this you wanted to know." But in a large blossom he was living. That deceased chief and three other chiefs were living in blossoms that were standing one after the other. "Thanks," said the Kwanitaka, "these were never bad in Oraibi: they were always good, therefore they are here this way now. Now, then, let us go and look there, too." So they again entered. There all kinds of grasses and plants and blossoms of every description were. "Thus these are living here," said the Kwanitaka. "This you wanted to know, hence now you took well. When you return you tell them. You see if any one is not wicked there in Oraibi he shall certainly come here. Here you have seen it. You see, there a road has been prepared for them. Now as soon as you arrive you tell them everything about this our life here, and if some one thinks to himself (has his welfare at his heart) he must live accordingly. Thus you wanted it. Because you have entered our dwelling, here everywhere you have found out everything, but as soon as you think of coming here sometime, you must eat a little of your medicine again, but you must tell this to your mother and your father and to them, but they must never do that way, and if they do not believe my talk they shall never live with us here. Now then, proceed. Run fast, as your father and mother are waiting for you."

Now then, from there he ran very fast. He arrived at the Kwanmongwi, where the road divided. He said to him, "Have you come?" "Yes," the young man said. "Very well," he replied, "run fast now, your father and mother are waiting for you." He now came running very fast. At Aoatovi he again came upon them who were being punished there, those who because they had stolen. They were going to the Skeleton House, but were still punished there, but they were concerned that their thieving should come to an end, and then sometime they might arrive at them in the Skeleton House. Now when he came upon them the one that was sitting there said to him: "So you have come back again!" "Yes," the young man replied, and at once proceeded, running very fast. Now he came upon the woman. She said, "So you have come back again!" "Yes," he answered, and upon that proceeded, running very fast.

He now came upon the one that had killed some one, north of Apohnivi. "So you have come back again," said the one that was punished there, "Yes," he answered. Having said this, he proceeded, running. Now he arrived a little north of Apohnivi. Now there the one that did not want it to rain was sitting. He also said the same thing. "Yes," the young man said, and proceeded, running. Now he arrived at his house in Oraibi and entered his body. Now when the sun was rising he awoke and sat up. He was thinking. The sun was somewhat high already. Now his mother, because she was through making the food, came to look after him and he had awoke. "Are you awake?" the mother said, "Yes," he replied. "Come then, let us eat; come this way," the mother said. "Very well," answered the young man. So they were eating. When they had eaten the father asked the young man: "Now what have you found out?" "Yes," he said, "yes, truly they are living. I have seen everything there in the Skeleton House and there the chief told me thus, thus I tell you. There that Kwanmongwi burns these wicked ones there, and these others he throws into the dark, and then again, these that have been chiefs here they live well there and they are chiefs there again. I have seen their way of living there. So when some time you will not see me here, you must not worry over that; truly they are living there." Thus he told them. And after that they were living together. By and by the young man wanted to go back again, and he said to his father, "My father, my mother." they said. "I shall go back again," he answered. "Very well," said the father, and that night he took some of that medicine and then slept, but now he was really dead. And (in the morning) the mother, in order that he should eat, in order that he should refresh himself, looked after her boy, but he had died. Now they wrapped him up and put him away, there below Kuivo. There they buried him.

After that they lived (alone), but they, the father and the mother, were homesick after their boy.

Now the father went to his field, and when he came there he hoed his field. Then at the edge of the field something was running. It was a bird, a Bachro. Now the Bachro spoke. "Alas!" he said, "alas, my father is homesick after me." "Yes," the father said, "I am homesick after you." The Bachro said, "Now you must not be that way; why I told you (all about it). In four days I shall come back again, hence you must both come." Having said this he flew away. Now, after four days the father said to the mother: "Let us go together." "Very well," she said. Now his wife prepared some lunch and then they left. When they arrived there they were making the field. Now the husband said to his wife, "Now somebody will come." "Who?" she asked. When they were still thus talking it arrived. Close by them something was whistling, and now he came running towards them and arrived at them. As soon as he had arrived at them he said, "Alas, you are homesick after me." Now the father said, "Yes." "Now you must not be that way," he said. "I live well." Now the mother said: "Yes, I am homesick after you." Now again he said, "You must not be that way. I shall come and see you. Having said this he again flew away. In the evening they went home and surely after that when the father was walking in the field that came there. After that they continued to live there.

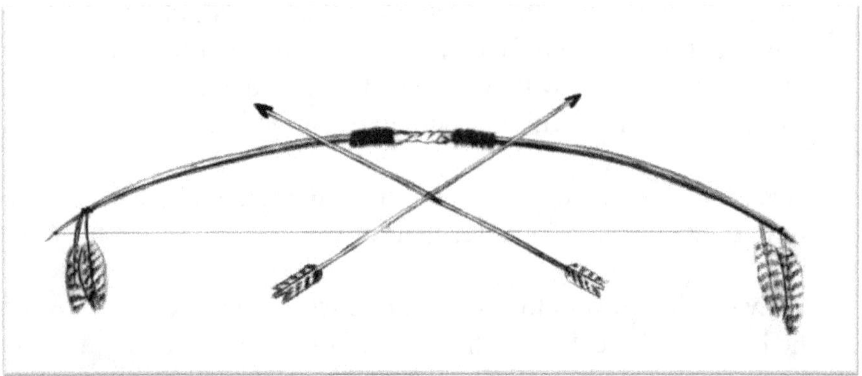

Skeleton Woman and the Hunter

Told by Sik'ahpik'i (Shupaulavi)

Aliksai! A long time ago the people were living in Mishongnovi, where now are the old ruins of the ancient village of Mishongnovi. In the village lived a very poor youth by the name of Kochoilap Tiyo (Fire-Keeping-Up-Youth), though just why he was called that way the tale does not say. He would usually sit in a corner of the kiva. When the people were spinning they would throw away the little pieces of impure wool that they picked from their piles of wool, and of these the youth mentioned had finally made himself a bed, on which he would sleep.

One time when it was winter and very cold, there was snow on the ground. The young men of the village were on the hunt, while the older men were in the kiva. They asked the youth why he had not gone along on the hunt. "Yes," he said, "I have no moccasins." "Well, you ought to be with them on the hunt," they said. "But I have no moccasins here," he replied again. The old men said, "You go into the houses and perhaps you will find a sheep pelt hanging before an opening. Bring that here." So he went and found one and brought it into the kiva. They soaked it in water and made him a pair of moccasins. They then sent the youth to find an old piece of blanket (no'mo), of which they made him some leggings or socks. After he had wrapped up his feet and had put on his moccasins they gave him an old patched blanket, which he also put on and tied a string around the blanket for a belt. They then gave him a bow and arrows and some throwing sticks. Hereupon they explained to him all about the difference between the rabbit tracks and those of other animals, as he had never been on the hunt before.

So he left the village and commenced to hunt. By and by he could hear the shoutings of the other hunters and he went in their direction. Soon he saw tracks in the snow and began to think that perhaps this is a rabbit track. He saw where the rabbit had been sitting and so he finally concluded that he had discovered the tracks of the rabbit and followed them for a long distance. Some of the hunters who had found something began to return home, but he followed the tracks. Finally he came upon a jack-rabbit who was very tired. Him he killed and he was so happy over his first game that he stroked the rabbit for quite a while. He then tied a string to its legs, and taking it on his back he thought of returning. It was getting dark and it commenced to rain. He started back, and after having traveled for some distance it was very dark and he came to a bluff where there was a place called Kawaylova. Here he saw a light, and coming nearer he found a kiva and looking in he noticed a pretty woman in the kiva. He was by this time wet and very cold. She invited him to come in, so he went in.

He sat down at the fireplace and warmed himself. She then gave him some pikami and oongawa to eat, but he discovered that the first was prepared of the brain of corpses and the other of flies, so although he was very hungry he did not eat anything. While he pretended to eat something he dropped the food in front of himself before he put it into his mouth. His rabbit he had left outside. He went and got it and handed it to the woman, who was Skeleton Woman. She was very happy over it and thanked him for it. She then said to him: "I am going to dance, and when I am through dancing we shall go to sleep together. You keep up the fire for me while I am dancing." Hereupon she went into another chamber of the kiva. While the young man was sitting at the fireplace he looked up and saw that the opening of the kiva was closed with many threads that were stretched across the opening in every direction. "How shall I get out of this?" he thought to himself, but just then he happened to think that he had a very small knife with him. This he drew out and began to sharpen it. Then the woman came out again and danced, singing the following song:

Mamanhoymuiyuu, mamanhoymuiyuu,
The maidens, the maidens.
Mucunkuy amuyu [Archaic].
Hokwae, hokwae.

But she was no longer the handsome woman, she now was a skeleton with exposed teeth and thin, bony legs.

When she turned around, while dancing, the youth jumped up, ran up the ladder, cut the strings with which the opening was closed, and ran away, the woman shouting after him, "Oh, my husband!" After running a distance the youth again came to a bluff called Cituhoilawhka. Here he again saw a light and approaching it he found another kiva. Looking in he saw a lively dance in progress. "Come in," some one said to him, so he entered. "Hide me quickly," he said to the dancers, "somebody is pursuing me," for the Skeleton Woman had followed him. "All right," they said, "come in quickly, dress up and dance with us," These were the crickets (nanakanchorzhtu). They took some soaked clay, rubbed it over his body, and prepared him as one of the dancers. So he was dancing along and they were singing the following song as they danced:

Hanatoili hanatoili,
Hanatoili hanatoili
Yamushkiki, yamushkiki,
Ruk! ruk!
(Meaning obsolete.)

All at once Skeleton Woman arrived at the entrance, and looking in, shouted: "How, how, is my husband not here?" but they danced on, pretending not to hear her. "He certainly must be here," she said. "I am going to come in." So she entered and examined the dancers and going through the crowd, hunted for the youth. While she was hunting one of the dancers whispered to the youth to run out now. This he did, running towards the village. The Skeleton Woman again followed him but failed to overtake him. He was very much frightened when he arrived at the village. For a long time he said very little, but was sitting quietly at his place in the kiva.

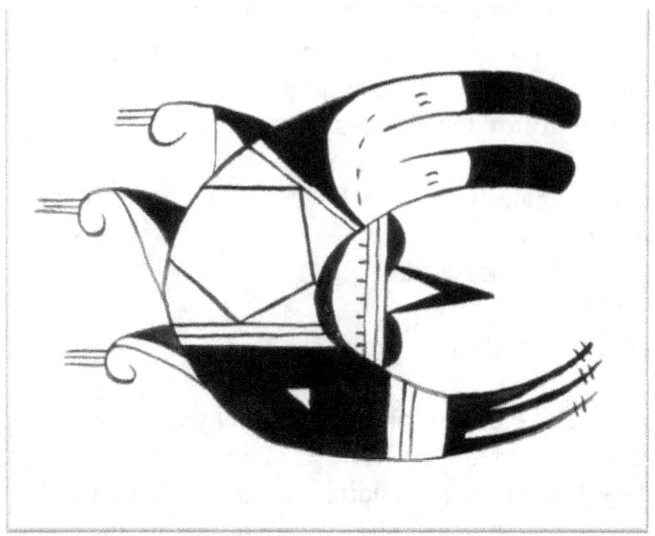

The Two Pueblo Maidens Who Were Married to the Night

Told by Lomanomtiwa (Oraibi)

Haliksai! In Kawaihkaa, a Pueblo village in New Mexico, the people were living. North of the plaza, at the house where there was a long ladder, lived two maidens. They were sisters, and persistently refused to marry any of the young men in the village. Finally the Night (Tokila) concluded to try to marry the two maidens, and came to the house. He came there in the evening and asked them to marry him. They said they would lay the matter before their parents, and if they were willing they would marry him. The parents were willing, and so the two sisters waited for their suitor. The next evening he came to fetch his two brides.

Leaving the village they went through a narrow passage. Outside of the village they found a large tray (pota), which the Night had left there. "This we shall enter," he said. So they all took a place on the tray, whereupon they were lifted up and carried through the air to Kawaihka Nuwatok'aovi, where they entered a deep canyon or gulch. Here the Night lived. When they came into the house they saw in an inner room a great many human bones. They were the remains of many women whom the Night had stolen in the village, and with whom he had lived a while and then, as soon as they became pregnant, had thrown them into the room to perish. A number of women and maidens were still living, and they pitied these two new arrivals, and said: "Alas! that you two have come with him." So the two were very unhappy.

Close by was a lake from which the two sisters used to get water. They stayed with the Night a while, but soon became very unhappy when they saw that they were pregnant. One time the younger sister went to get some water and then somebody spoke to her. It was the Frog. "You poor one," he said, "You must go home this night. Here is a large trail. In the evening you must take your water jars on your head and come after water. You leave them here, and then you follow this road, which leads to your home. This you must tell your sister also." Hereupon the younger sister returned and said to her older sister: "There at the water some one has told me something." "What did he say to you?" she asked. "He told me that we should go home this night."

So in the evening, after they had eaten, they took their water jars and went after water. When they arrived at the lake the Frog said: "Have you come'" "Yes," they replied. "Very well, you just follow this track, and you trot, and you will arrive at your home." After they had traveled a distance they came upon Spider Woman, who was sitting close to the trail in a stooping position as an old hag. "Have you come?" she said. "Yes," they replied. "Very well, I have heard that you are going home, and so I waited for you here." She then told them that she would go along, and that they should not fear. So they traveled on that night and did not sleep any. The next day, when they had traveled until about noon, Spider Woman looked back and saw some clouds approaching. "They are coming," she said: "and will certainly overtake us."

The three did not tarry, but when they had come nearly to the village the sky was full of clouds; they had overtaken them. When they had arrived close to the village they were struck by lightning and killed. But as they were killed, each one was delivered of a child, the elder sister of a little boy, the younger one of a little girl. The children remained alive and at once began to nurse. During the night their mothers would become alive, but during the day they were always dead. In that way the children were brought up. Finally they began to walk around. Spider Woman had left the two fugitives as soon as they were struck by lightning.

When the children had grown up somewhat, they asked their mothers who their father was. "We certainly have a father, and you tell us who he is, and we will go to him; then he will take care of us and provide for us." The mothers then told them, "Yes, you have a father, but from him we have fled, and he will not care for you. East of here is a village, Kawaihkaa, and there is where we used to live. There our father and our mother live. You go there and north of the plaza where the big ladder is you inquire and see what they will say to you. There is where we used to live. But they too are bad. They will undoubtedly ask you to contend with them, and if any one is beaten they usually kill him. On top of the ladder something is hanging, and if any one does not guess that, he is killed; but if they contend with you and beat you, you must guess that. There is a little turtle tied up in it."

Hereupon they slept until morning, then the two children started. Their mothers said to them: "If they contend with you and your grandfather pities you and gives you something, you bring us something too, so that we can dress up, because our clothes are worn out. If they do not say anything to you, we shall go there too." When they arrived at the village they crossed the plaza, saw the ladder, and went up. Their grandparents lived in a kiva there. They entered and sat down. The grandparents had always been sad and sorry and at first did not say anything. Finally the grandfather saw them and asked, "Who are you?" "Why, it is we," they said. "But who are you? Where do you come from?" "From west of here," they replied. "From Akokovi (a village west of Kawaihkaa)?" the grandfather asked. "No," they said, "not from there, but we stayed right west of here." "But who are you?" they asked again.

"A long time ago you had two daughters and somebody fetched them, and we are their children. We have grown up now and have come here." Hereupon they set food before them and fed them. The grandmother was crying. When they had eaten, sure enough, they were asked to play a game with them. "If they are our grandchildren," they said, "they will know something." So the grandfather laid out a flat stone on which was drawn a tu'kwnanawohpi. The grandfather sat on one side, the boy at the other end, and then they began to play. The boy won the game. "Very well," the grandfather said, "there at the top of the ladder something is wrapped up. You guess what that is. If you guess that you kill me, and if you do not guess it I shall kill you." Hereupon they all went out and looked at the bundle that was hanging at the top of the ladder. "Now, what is in there?" the grandfather said. "Who knows?" the child said. "You guess once," the brother said to his sister. "How do I know what can be in there?" she said; "you guess." "Now, do not hesitate," the grandfather said, "but speak out and say what you think." "Why, what can be in there?" the little brother finally said; "it is perhaps a little turtle." "Now, you are surely our grand-children," the grandfather exclaimed.

"Well now, you kill me," the grandfather said. "No, we do not want to kill you," the children replied, "but you pay us something." "Very well," the grandfather said, "what do you want?" "I want a shirt, a how, and quiver with arrows, and some wrist protectors, and a pair of moccasins," the boy said. The little girl asked for a dress, a blanket, moccasins, and a belt. And thus the grandparents paid them these things. They then also asked for some clothes; for their mothers, whereupon the grandfather gave them four sheep-wool dresses, two pairs of moccasins, and two belts. The children then said, that their mothers had said, if they were willing and would not say anything, then the mothers would also come. "Certainly you must come," the grandparents said; "you shall not remain there," So the children took these things with them and returned to their mothers.

When they arrived there the latter were very happy. The little boy was already shooting his arrow. They all dressed up now and ate their evening meal. Hereupon they proceeded to the village, but all abreast. In this same manner they ascended the ladder, and when they had arrived at the opening the elder woman called down, "Our father, our mother," but received no answer. The younger sister then called down the same words, but received no answer. "They do not care for us," they said. The children had told their grandparents that their mothers would come if the grandparents would not say anything to them. They then descended the ladder and stopped at the elevated portion in the kiva. Again the two called, "Our father, our mother," and again no answer. "They do not care for us," the two women said. They then descended into the deeper portion of the kiva and again one after the other called, "Our father, our mother," whereupon the grandmother responded. "How!" she said, and immediately her two children and two grandchildren fell dead. Had they heeded the injunction a little better, and had been quiet just once more, the fourth time they would all have lived together happily, but this way now they had no children.

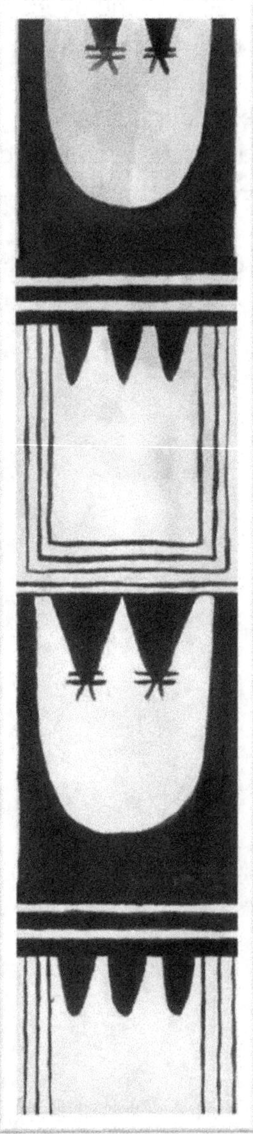

How Hiyonatitiwa Defeated the Plan of His Enemies

Told by Lomanomtiwa (Oraibi)

Haliksai! In Oraibi they were living. At the place where now Hongsi and Nakwsu live, lived a maiden who refused all offers of marriage. The young men of the village would frequently go there and try to win her affections, but without success. At Achamali (now a shrine a few hundred yards north of the village) lived a youth by the name of Hiyonatitiwa, with his grandmother. They were very poor. The young man always went around with a patched blanket, and his grandmother also did so. One time he said to the latter: "My grandmother!" "Ha!" she said. "I am going to go south to that maiden there and see whether she will not marry me." "O my!" the grandmother said, "you are so poor, she will certainly not want you, and you are thinking of it. But at least go there and try it," she said to him.

So one time he came to the village. On the Snake and Flute and other kivas and on some of the houses the young men were still sitting, as it was twilight. As they saw the youth come they said: "Aha, somebody is coming here." So he stood and waited. They went to their supper and then returned, taking their previous places again. But the young man, not wanting to wait any longer, boldly passed between them to the house of the maiden. There was an open window in the upper story of the house, and to this the youth went up. The young people who saw him smiled. The maiden was grinding corn, but occasionally stopped. The young people watched the proceedings, and as they heard that the maiden occasionally stopped grinding, they concluded and said that the young man must be welcome, and she must be talking with him sometimes, because she stops grinding corn occasionally.

The young man talked to the maiden and asked her to marry him. She said that if her father and mother were willing, she would marry him. "Very well," he said, he would return the next evening, and if they were willing he would fetch her. Hereupon he returned home. The young men of the village were very unhappy. The youth said to his grandmother that to-morrow he would fetch the maiden. She refused to believe it. "Certainly I am going to fetch her," he said. And so the day passed and evening came. When it was dark he again proceeded to the house of the maiden. The young men of the village were again sitting on the roofs of the kivas and houses watching him. He went up to the house, and after a little while brought with him the mana, taking her to his house. The young men said to him as they passed along: "So you are fetching her. What do you want with her? But, of course, you are going to dress her up in patched blankets."

So he brought her to the house of his grandmother and went in. She took charge of the maiden and the latter remained there. The next three days she ground corn, and on the morning of the fourth day the grandmother washed their heads, but there was nobody there to participate. There was nobody there to make a bridal costume, for which the maiden was now sorry. Hereupon the bride remained there and prepared the food for them, but no one prepared a bridal costume for her. When she had remained there about the time that brides usually remain at their husband's house before they go home to their mother's house, the old grandmother said: "Now, you have been here about that long, we shall see whether we can find something for you."

That day the young man went hunting and brought home a great deal of meat. They prepared some no'okwiwi, some pikami, etc. Of this they ate in the evening. Early the next morning the grandmother again washed the head of the bride, and hereupon she went into a room on the north side and was hunting around there, knocking things about, but found nothing. Going into another room on the west side she did the same, but had nothing when she came out. She repeated this in a room on the south side, but when she came out of a room on the east side she brought with her a complete bridal costume--two white robes, a pair of moccasins, a white, knotted, fringed belt and a reed receptacle. She dressed up the bride, sprinkled a road of corn-meal for her, and sent her home to her parents. The people were again sitting on their housetops and kiva roofs, and, behold! there the young bride came home, dressed as brides usually are dressed. When she came to her mother's house her mother was very happy.

Her husband went on a hunt the next day and brought back with him a mountain sheep. This he handed to his wife's parents, who were very happy over it. The inhabitants of the Snake and Nashabe kivas were very angry at this young man and were planning how they could kill him. They decided to make a raid on the Navaho. But the father of the young wife was also one of the inhabitants of the Snake kiva, and so he found out how matters stood. He told his son-in-law about it, and the latter informed his grandmother. She said that the next morning he should send his wife's little sister to the Snake kiva to call his father-in-law for breakfast. Hereupon the young man returned.

In the morning the maiden went to the Snake kiva, called her father for the morning meal, and added that in four days there would be war, whereupon she ran back. The people in the kiva were surprised, but laughed. The next day she repeated this, saying that in three days there would be war, and soon. In the evening of the second day the father and his son-in-law went over to the old woman at Achamali, and said: "It is drawing nearer." "Yes," she said, "when they will have a race to-morrow you must not race with them, but you both come here first and start from here." Whereupon the two returned home. The next morning the little maiden repeated the same words. The men now began to feel uneasy, saving that that maiden certainly did not say that for nothing. Something must be about to happen.

On the morning of the third day she repeated the same words, saying: "To-morrow there will be war." That day the men made bows and arrows all day. On the morning of the fourth day the maiden again said: "Let us go and eat, but to-day there will be war," whereupon she ran home. It had been noised abroad that some Navaho were approaching the village and were attacking some men in the fields. The men who were not killed ran towards the village and shouted. The men of the village at once got ready and descended the village to meet the Navaho raiders. Hiyonatitiwa and his father-in-law each got two quivers full of arrows and a bow, and then ran over to Achamali to the old woman's house. "Have you come"' she said. "Yes," they replied. Hereupon she went to the room on the north and called in: "Come out here, your grandchildren have come here." At once somebody came. It was the Puma. She then called into the room on the west side: "Your grandchildren have come, come out here," and a Bear came out. She repeated this, calling into the room on the south side, and a Wildcat came out. Repeating this same act on the east side, a Wolf came out of the room.

While this was going on at Achamali, the Hopi had met the Navaho, and the latter were constantly asking where Hiyonatitiwa was. "He is in the village yet," the Hopi replied. "Go and get him, he is slow," the Navaho said. By this time the young man and his father-in-law, accompanied by the four animals, descended the mesa. The animals at once rushed upon the Navaho, who were nearly all killed, and also the Hopi that had planned this raid in order to get Hiyanatitiwa out of the way, and then steal his wife. When those who remained alive returned to the village there was a great deal of mourning there. "Somebody has certainly brought this about that some of our people have now been killed also," they said. And this way it was prevented that some one should take away the Young man's wife, and he forever afterwards lived with her.

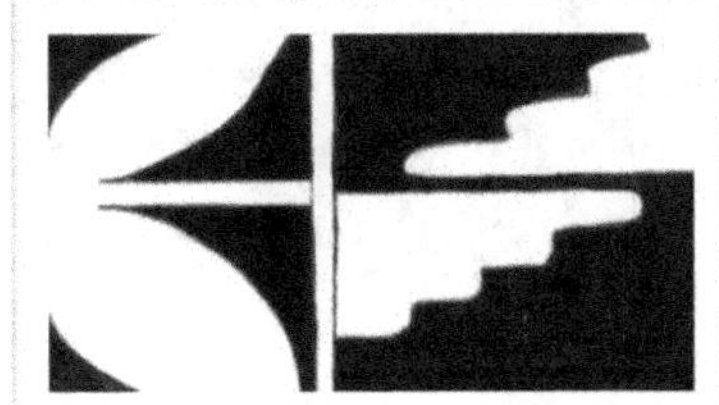

The Shongopavi Maiden Who Turned Into a Dog

Told by Moho (Oraibi woman)

Haliksai! In Shongopavi they were living, and a youth there was very handsome, and all the maidens were coveting him. And one maiden was young yet, had small hair whorls; she was dirty, and a bad looking maiden. The maidens owned the chiro birds, and one of the maidens ground coarse meal (hakwushkwi) for them and put it into a tray, and when she had put it in she lifted it up, and while she was singing she threw it away. She sang: "Pota, pota, pota, Yoa ini, yoa ini," and then scattered it to the birds. Now the chiros darted towards it and ate of it, and when they had eaten they dispersed again, whistling, and were flying around somewhere in the field. When it was evening they again assembled at the mana's house. In the morning she again made hakwushkwi for them and fed them, and after that the mana always fed them.

Now that youth also made a tray. When he was done with it the maidens assembled. He handed that tray to them, and when he had handed it to them he said: "Now then, who opens this shall get me." Now one when she had loosened it could not untie it. She handed it to another one, who could not untie it, and thus one after the other tried to loosen and untie it, and not one could open it. Now then, when it came to that bad looking maiden she also tried it. Now the old grandmother (Spider Woman) informed her, "When you will sing this you will open it." Thus she informed her. So the maiden, while she was secretly singing, opened it. When she had opened it, singing secretly, she opened it as her song ended. When she had opened it all she owned the youth. Then those pretty maidens were very sad and were angry.

Now the youth took her to his house, where the mother of the youth bathed her entirely, whereupon she became a pretty maiden. She now remained there as a bride. Then they made a bridal costume for her whereupon she went home. When she went home the youth followed her. Now she slept there in their house twice, and when she slept there the second time she did not get up. At last when they were eating they would still not get up, so the mother of the maiden went up to them and looked at them and they were still sleeping, but that maiden had turned into something; she had turned into a dog. Now the mother said to them, "Get up, please." The dog got up at once and rushed out right away and jumped down as a dog, and at once ran away somewhere, and is still going around somewhere.

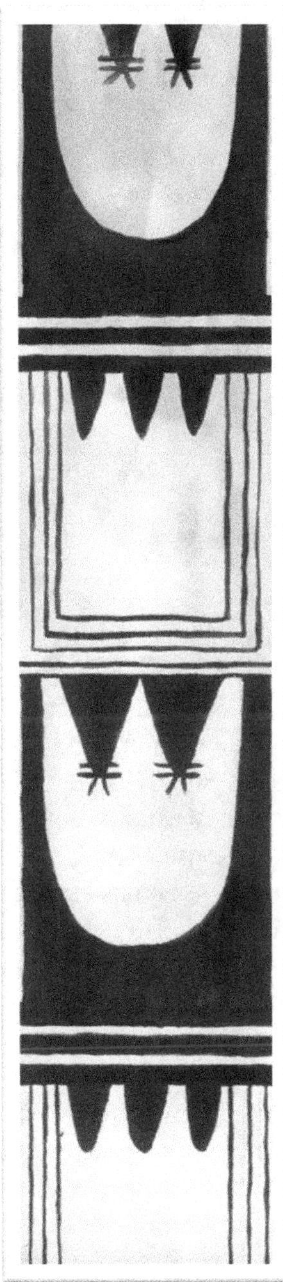

Big Head and Goat Horn

Haliksai! In Oraibi they were living. East of the Kwan kiva a youth lived, by the name of Big Head (Wuyakqoto), away south are the Hopi Buttes, and on the westernmost butte lived Goat Horn (Chiwakala). These two were friends, but as they lived so far apart they did not visit each other often; but one time Goat Horn visited his friend in Oraibi. After they had eaten and talked together, towards evening Goat Horn wanted to return home. "My friend," he said to Big Head. "What is it?" the latter replied. "You must come and visit me sometime, too," Goat Horn said; whereupon he went home. After a while Big Head visited his friend, and stayed all night there. In the morning Goat Horn killed a goat for his friend, cut it in two, and gave him one-half, which Big Head took with him to the village; and that is the reason why Hopi, when they kill a goat, cut it up.

Kavushkavuwnom and Shovivioun om

Told by Lomanomtiwa And Tangakhoyoma (Oraibi)

Haliksai! In Oraibi they were living. At Bayavushtuhco lived a woman by the name of Kavushkavuwnom, and at Oanmuru lived a woman by the name of Shoviviounom. These two women were great friends. They usually got water at Spider Spring (Kohkangva). One time Kavushkavuwnom was getting water again, and as she was returning her friend Shoviviounom met her, also getting water. The latter asked her in a half-singing manner: "What now [in order] to cook, you get water?" (Hihta vula kwiwanikae kuyito?) Whereupon Kavushkavuwnom replied: "A dish of young squashes" (Ngamoochona). Shoviviounom hereupon said: "So you are going to feast?" (Aha, halihi kurzh pas um chonni?) "Yes," the other one replied, "you must come this evening and visit me," whereupon they separated, the one going home with her water, and the other one going after water.

When Shoviviounom returned with her water she went to grinding corn and prepared some hurushuki. Of this she put some into a tray and proceeded to the house of her friend, Kavushkavuwnom, who had invited her to come over. The latter had in the meanwhile prepared her dish of young squashes. This she put into a bowl and the two then sat down and ate the squashes and the hurushuki. While they were eating they conversed together, and when they were through and Shoviviounom had visited for a little while, she returned to her home.

The next morning Shoviviounom went after water first. She looked around several times for her friend, who, however, was not yet coming. She went down to the spring, filled her jug with water, but still her friend was not coming. So she returned to the village, and as she was ascending the incline to the village Kavushkavuwnom descended from the village, also going after water. When they met, Kavushkavuwnom asked her friend: "What now [in order] to cook, you get water?" (Hihta vula kwiwanikae kuyito?) Whereupon Shoviviounom replied: "Tavochona.".. So you are going to feast?" "(Aha, halihi kurzh pas um chonni?) Kavushkavuwnom said. "Yes," Shoviviounom replied, "you must come and visit me in the evening. "

When they had both returned they prepared their meals, Kavushkavuwnom preparing some hurushuki, and Shoviviounom preparing a dish of rabbit meat. In the evening Kavushkavuwnom proceeded to the house of her friend. The latter put her dish of rabbit meat into a bowl, and Kavushkavuwnom added her hurushuki. The two then ate, enjoying their feast. When they were through, they conversed together until the sun went down, whereupon Kavushkavuwnom returned to her house and both retired for the night.

How the Children of Pivanhonk'api Obtained Permission to Catch Birds

Told by Kwayeshva (Oraibi)

Haliksai! At Hu'kovi they were living, and at Pivanhonk'api they were also living. At both places there were a great many children, and they always went down to Mumushva (a spring named after a certain herb and grass that grows in the spring), where they were setting bird traps. They were often at enmity with one another on account of the birds. One morning they again went to trap birds. They again became very angry at one another on account of the trapping, and the Hu'kovi children said to the children of Pivanhonk'api that they should not trap birds there. But they said if they would give them something they could trap birds there. So the children from Pivanhonk'api ran back to the village and got such things as kutu'ki, piki, and different other articles of food, and gave them to the children of Hu'kovi, so that the latter carried home a great deal of food which they had purchased for the permission given to the Pivanhonkapi children to catch birds there, and after that the children from both villages were always catching birds there, and maybe they are catching birds there still.

The Jug Boy

Told by Tangakhoyoma (Oraibi)

In the village of Hano the people were living. The Hano know how to make the earthen jugs, and one time a handsome young woman also made an earthen jug. She kneaded the clay and when her hands were tired she trampled it with her feet, so that the wet clay spurted all around. By and by this woman bore a child, but it was an earthen jug, inside of which was a little boy, who cried when he was born. The women who were present were happy. "Ishuni!" they said, "you have borne a child," whereupon they washed the jug child, and in that way the child grew up. But the mother nursed it, holding her breast over the opening of the jug when the child nursed.

By and by the child grew up and began to talk like the Hano, and from that time on the child refused to take the mother's breast; it asked for some food, and from there on it ate food which the mother put into the jug. Thus the child grew to be a young man. One time it rained and then it snowed, and the young men then went hunting. In the evening they came home carrying the rabbits. That jug youth envied them. He had a grandfather, and said to the grandfather, "My grandfather." "Hay!" the latter replied. "I want to go hunting, too." "Very well," he replied, and then the grandfather made a bow for him and arrows, and tied feathers to the arrows, and when he had made them he tied them to the jug handles. He also tied some food to the jug and a burden band with it. These things he made.

Then the grandfather lifted the jug up, carried it down from the village and left it there. He said to him, "Now go on; there in the field they are hunting, hence when you proceed and find rabbit tracks somewhere you follow them. This kind of tracks they have," whereupon he drew them for him. Now then he (the jug youth) moved forward in a wabbling manner and descended somewhere along the path. When he had descended he went somewhere northward from the village. Then he moved up and down that way, and sure enough somewhere found some tracks. He followed them and there, sure enough, a rabbit was running. Now that jug youth moved very fast, so that the mouth of the jug whistled. He circled around the rabbit once, then the rabbit jumped into the wash. The jug youth also came and jumped down. When he landed on the ground he burst into two and a Hopi came bouncing out of it.

After that he at once untied the bow and arrows and burden band. He now took the burden band, the bow and arrows, and followed the rabbit. The rabbit became tired and sat down. When the youth found him he shot it. He then followed another one and killed it. Thus he killed four. He now tied them up and carried them on his back and then went home from there. When it was evening he came to his mother carrying the rabbits, and she was truly happy. "Oh my! Thanks that you have killed them, thanks, thanks," she said. The grandfather now also said: "Thanks, thanks, why you have fixed yourself up somewhere, and hence you are now a Hopi and have carried these here to me. Thanks! Why now subsisting on your account I shall live here." When he had thus spoken to him, after that that one lived as a Hopi, and after that he always provided something for his mother, and then subsisting on his account (by his assistance) they lived there.

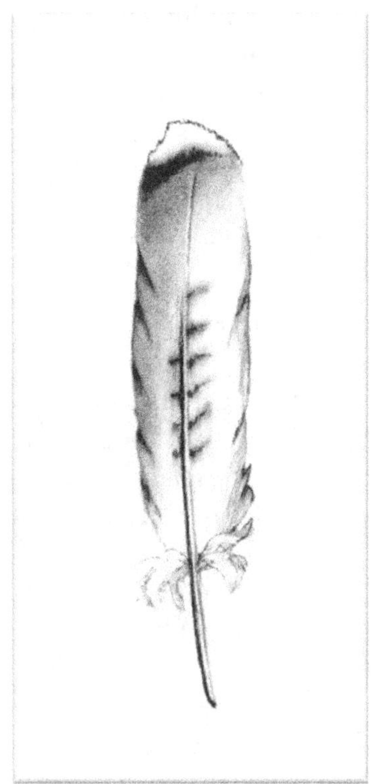

Muyingwa, Two Children, and the Hummingbird

Told by Qoyawaima (Oraibi)

A long time ago the Oraibi had nothing to eat as it did not rain for about four or five years. The first year the corn became large enough so that some corn-ears just began to ripen, then the frost came and killed it. The next year the ears were just forming when the frost again killed the corn. The third year the ears did not even begin to form when the stalks were killed by frost. The fourth year it remained very small. The people by this time had eaten all the corn they had saved from previous years and some began to move away. Some of them, however, still planted some the fifth year, but the drought was so great that the corn withered soon after it had come out of the ground.

They all left then, trying to find something to eat with other people. Only a little boy and his sister were left in the village. One time the little brother made a little bird for his sister from the pith of the sunflower stalk and gave it to her to play with. While he went away to hunt something else for her she played with the little bird, throwing it upwards several times, and all at once it became a living Hummingbird and flew away. When the boy returned he asked her what she had done with her little bird. She told him that it had flown away, at which he was very much surprised. The children had hardly anything to eat. The next morning the little bird came back, flew into the house where the children stayed and entered an opening in one of the walls. "My little bird has come back!" the little girl said. "Where is it?" the boy asked. "Why, it went into that opening there." The boy put his hand into the opening and found that it seemed to be very large. The bird he could not find, but he found a little corn-ear which the bird had apparently placed there. At this the children were very glad. They broke it in two, roasted it, and ate it. Soon the bird came out of the opening and flew away again. The next day it returned with a larger corn-ear which the children ate, and so it returned for four days, always bringing a larger corn-ear for the children. On the fifth day it came back but did not bring any corn with it. When the boy reached into the opening he drew forth the little bird, but in the form in which he had made it. He held it in his hand and said: "You are something living. You go and hunt our parents, they have left us here and you will perhaps find them, and you bring us something to eat. You go south here and look for our father and mother. "

Hereupon the boy asked his sister how she had caused the bird to fly. She took the little bird by the wings and said: "This is the way I did it," throwing it upward, whereupon the bird was alive again and flew away. Sitting upon a rock south of the village the little bird looked southward and all at once detected at Tu'wanashabe, a cactus plant with a single red blossom. The bird at once flew towards this plant and removing it found an opening under it. Entering this opening it found itself in a kiva where some grass and herbs were growing. At the north end of this kiva was another opening. Passing through this one, the little bird found itself in a second kiva. Here it found some corn with some pollen on it, and ate some of it. At the north end of this kiva there was also an opening leading into a third kiva. Entering this kiva the bird found grass, herbs, and corn of all kinds, and here also lived Mu'yingwa, the God of Growth and Germination.

There were also all kinds of birds in this last kiva, but it was the Humming-birds that first noticed the little intruder and told Mu'yingwa about it. "Somebody has come in," they said. "Who is it?" he asked, "and where is he? Let him come here." So the little bird flew on Mu'yingwa's arm and waited. "Why are you going about here?" Mu'yingwa asked. "Yes," the bird said, "what are you doing here? Why have you listened to the wishes of the bad people who wanted you to retire here to this place and not concern yourself about the people up there? Why have you complied with their wishes? Your fields up there look very bad. It has not rained there and nothing is growing. The people have all left except two poor little children who are the only ones left in Oraibi. You come out here and look after things up there." "All right," Mu'yingwa answered, "I am thinking about the matter."

Hereupon the bird asked for something to eat and also for something to bring to those children, saying that they had not had anything that day, and that they were hungry. Mu'yingwa told the bird to take just what it wanted and bring it to the children. So the bird broke off a nice roasting corn-ear to take along. Arriving at the house it flew into the same opening again, disposing of the corn-ear there. The boy reached into the opening and drew forth the corn-ear. The children were very happy over it and talked to the bird, which was still in the opening, and said: "Thank you that you have pitied us, thank you that you have brought us something to eat again. On your account we live here now. Through you we can satisfy our hunger. We are very happy over it. You must not leave us now." The bird answered: "Yes, I have pity on you and for that reason I have come again. I shall now live close by here, at Tu'wanashabe."

The children then asked the bird to hunt for their parents, and so the bird flew away to hunt for them. Flying over the fields west of Oraibi it proceeded towards the north, and at a place called Toho (from a black shale or paint gotten from there by the Hopi to this day), it found the father and the mother of these children. They were living upon some cactus that was growing there, but were very much emaciated. When the Humming-bird flew by them the man said: "Something is passing by here," but looking around they could not see anything, so the bird came back and was then detected by the man and his wife. The man at once went towards the bird, saying: "Who are you, flying about here?" The bird stopped in its flight, though keeping its wings in motion and listened to what the man had to say. He asked the little bird to pity them and procure them some food. There was no living being in that part of the country at that time, and so from the fact that this bird was flying about there the people concluded that it must know some place where it found something to eat. The bird did not answer anything, but flew away. Arriving at the opening in the children's house, the boy asked: "Did you find our parents?" "Yes," the Humming-bird answered," away up north I found them." "Both of them?" the children asked. "Yes, both of them," the bird replied; "but alas, they have very little to eat. They are hungry and they are very much emaciated."

The children then begged the bird to bring them something to eat, whereupon it flew away. Mu'yingwa had in the meanwhile concluded to go up into the world and look after things there. He first ascended to the first kiva above him, where he stayed four days. During this time it rained a little about Oraibi. After four days he ascended into the next kiva above him when it rained again on the earth. He then ascended into the third kiva, whereupon it rained considerably in and around Oraibi, and when he after four more days emerged from the last kiva he found that the grasses and herbs were growing nicely.

The parents of the children had seen from the distance the clouds and rain about Oraibi, and concluded to return to the village, not knowing that their children were still living. Others of the inhabitants of Oraibi who had not yet perished, also heard that it was now raining at their village and so they also returned. When these children grew up they, and after them their descendants, became the village chiefs and owners of the village of Oraibi.

(The informant says that this tale is not complete. He says that he knows it is longer, but he has forgotten some of the details about it.)

The Kalatoto Who Wished To Have Hair on His Head

Told by Kwayeshva (Oraibi)

Haliksai! At Kutukwuhschomo (so called after a certain kind of grass, Kutukwuhci, that grew on that hill), used to live a Kalatoto. In' the village of Oraibi lived many people. Kalatoto would often visit the village and try to find something to eat among the refuse near the village. The children of the village, finding the Kalatoto would tease and worry him, snapping their finger nails against his head, so that sometimes he would almost die. He would then retire to his house again. This happened very often and the Kalatoto was thinking how he could get some hair at least on the head, like the Hopi children had, who otherwise were just as nude as the Kalatoto. He had no hair nor any protection of any kind over his entire body. He finally concluded that he would go to the timber and get some pitch, which he did. Taking some of this pitch to his house he went to the village to hunt some hair that had been thrown on the piles of refuse by the Hopi, and finding some, he took it to his house and was very happy.

The next morning he put some of the pitch on his head and pasted some hair on it, so that he now had hair like the Hopi children. He was now very happy and made a visit to the village again. The children soon discovered him again and said: "Here is somebody," and one of the children soon recognized the Kalatoto, saying, "It seems to be the Kalatoto, but he has now hair." "It smells very much like pitch here," some of the children said, "he has put pitch on his head," and they at once took little sticks and putting one end of them on his head the pitch adhered to the sticks. As the Hopi children are very fond of pitch they began to chew the pitch, scraping all off of his head.

He was very sorry and returned to his home, gathering up, however, the hairs which the children had pulled out of the pitch and thrown away, and he took them along. He meditated about the matter all night, and in the morning went into the timber north of the village again. Finding some cactus, he took with him some of the juice to his house. In the morning he put some of this on his head and again pasted the hair to the juice, which adhered firmly after the juice had nearly dried.

So he went again to the village. The children seeing him said: "Here he has come again," and once more tried with little sticks to remove his head covering, but they soon found that this time it was not pitch. So he remained there a while, the children again worrying him. Towards evening he went home, and by that time the juice had dried so thoroughly that it began to crack and fall off with the hair. He was now again very unhappy.

At that time it was piki providing day (piktotok'a) in the village, preparatory for a Katcina dance. The Kalatoto was very unhappy, as he had hoped to attend the dance with the hair on his head. The next morning he again repaired to the woods to get some more pitch, which he found quickly. Bringing it to the house, he again felt happy, thinking that now he would have hair to attend the dance the next day. He was very happy and in the evening put some of the pitch on his head again, pasting new hair to it. He then retired and slept well that night. In the morning he heard the Katcinas dance and wanted to go to the village, but the pitch had gotten warm during the night and the hair and pitch adhered closely to the floor on which he had been sleeping. He made repeated efforts to rise, but could not. So he heard the Katcinas dance and sing all day, but could not get up. As he finally became very hungry and no one brought him anything to eat, he perished there.

The Child Who Turned Into an Owl

Told by Sik'ahpik'i (Shupaulavi)

Aliksai! They were living in Shupaulavi, and one time a child was crying bitterly. Its mother did not pity it and beat it. "You are crying," she said: "I am going to throw you out doors. I am going to throw you out to the Owl." Hereupon she dragged the child out of the house. A large Owl had been close by and had heard the moaning of the child. He came to the child and when he saw the latter still crying he put him on his back and carried him off. He lived in a little cave at the side of the bluff on which the village of Bayupki was situated. To this cave he took the child. The Owl had little children in the cave that were living there nicely.

When the mother of the child no longer heard the crying, she came out of the house and looked for her child, but it was gone. "Where has that child gone now?" she said. "It seems somebody came and got it," whereupon she went through the houses and inquired everywhere, but no one had it. In the morning she again went through the houses hunting her child, but could not find it, "Where may that child be?" she said. So she was without children.

Sometime after some men went after wood north of the village, some of them passing the cave where the Owl lived. They heard some one in a moaning voice sing the following song:

Chavayo chavayo,
Chavayo piva, chavayo piva,
A hmhm, a hmhm.

Looking up they saw a child in the cave, which had already feathers, and the white spots of the Owl began to appear all over the body. The eyes of the child also began to become yellow. "Oh!" the men said, "whose child may that be?" One of the men then suggested that it might be the child that had disappeared, so when they returned to the village they said: "There in the cave of an owl, at Bayupki, is a child. It already has feathers and spots all over, and its eyes are already yellow. It is turning into an owl. Whose child may that be?" "It must be the child of that woman," the people said right away, so they told them about it. "Now, bestir yourself, bestir yourself, because that child is turning into an owl." So they hurried up and the mother and father and the men who had found the child then proceeded to the place.

When they arrived there the men who had found the child climbed up to the cave. In the back part of the latter was the Owl and his children. The little owl child was sitting alone. The men took it, brought it down and handed it to its father. The mother also took hold of it. The Owl did not come out, but said: "You take the child with you, but when you get to your village you put the child into a room and keep it locked up there for four days. On the fourth day when the sun rises you open the door and let the child come out. It will then be a Hopi again. If you do not do that and open the door before that, the child will remain an Owl and come back again."

So they took the child to the village, put it into a room, placed some food in it and locked the door. The father watched in front of the door, keeping watch there during the four days. He heard his child move about in the room. After the first day the mother was anxious to open the door, but the father forbid her, saying that they were not to do that, because the Owl had forbidden it. So she waited and on the third day she was very anxious for her child and could hardly await the third day. During the night also, and it seemed to her as if the morning was very slow coming. Finally when it became light she went to the door, which, like the old Hopi doors, that were not made very well, had cracks. "It is light already," she said, "let us open the door." Hereupon she shaded her eyes and looked through one of the cracks. She saw her child walking up and down, but also noticed that it began to change into an owl again. "Let us open the door," she urged, "it is already light." Her husband protested, saying, that the sun had not yet risen, but she opened the door, and out rushed an Owl which immediately rose up and flew towards Bayupki to the place where it had come from. "Well, now," the man said, "there you looked in before the sun had risen, and yet the Owl had told us not to do so. You have done this, now you have done it and we have no children now. We were just getting our child back again, and now you looked in and it has turned into an Owl, and it will now remain an Owl."

The Children and the Lizards

Told by Sik'ahpik'i (Shupaulavi)

Aliksai! A long time ago the people lived in Mishongnovi. There was to be a dance in the village of Shongopavi and a man from Walpi was going to attend this dance. He came by way of Mishongnovi, which was then situated half-way down the mesa, where there are still the ruins of the old village. East of the village there was a large rock, and at this rock some children were playing. They were hunting some lizards, the kind that are called ha'kwa (pl. hakwahpu). "What are you doing there?" the Walpi man asked. "We are hunting these ha'kwas." "What are they?" he said. Why these here in the cracks and on the rocks," the children said. So some of the little boys got their bows and arrows ready and, aiming at some of the lizards, sang the following song:

Hakwa, puta ponongaqo
Lizard that, in the body.
Wihu qoiotak'ang,
Fat full of.
Aaay alihi alihi,
Nahanak nahanak hanak!

As they sang the last word they shot their arrows at the lizards.

From here the Walpi man proceeded westward towards Shongopavi. All at once he heard something, and standing still he listened and heard somebody say:

"Halaye, halaye.

He looked around for some time, but could not see anything. All at once he saw some little gray lizards. They were sitting upright and ejecting these peculiar sounds. The man looked down for a while, and saw how the lizards were running around and playing with on, another. Then, as he had lost so much time at the first place and also at this place, he gave up the visit to Shongopavi and returned. When he arrived at his home he related that he had not been to the dance, but that he had watched some children hunting, and that they had been singing the following song:

Machakwata ponongaqo,
Horned Lizard in body when
Wihu qoiotakang
Fat full of.
Aaay alihi, alihi,
Nahanak, nahanak hanak.

This song was forever afterwards spoken of as one of the Mishongnovi songs.

The Coyote and the Turtles

Told by Qoyawaima (Oraibi)

A long time ago the Turtles lived in a river called Blue River (Sakwabayu), somewhere south-east of Winslow (Homolovi). The Coyote was always hunting for something to eat. One time he was also hunting for food near the place where the Turtles lived. The latter would sometimes come out of the water and hunt cactus (yo'ngo) which they relished very much, and from which they have their name, Yongo'sona (pl. Yoyo'ngosontu).

One of the Turtles had a little baby Turtle. One time when they were all going to hunt food again, the Turtle said: "I am not going to take my child with me, because it is sleeping so nicely. I am going to bring a cactus back with me and give it to my child." After they had left, the little Turtle awoke, and when it found nobody there it asked, "Where is my mother?" and began to cry, and at once came out of the water. Looking for the tracks, it found that they led to the bank and then way off somewhere. It followed the tracks for some distance, but could not find any one, and so cried very bitterly. The Coyote, hearing the cries of the little Turtle, at once hunted it up and when he found it he said: "What are you singing? You are singing something very nice. Sing again." "I am not singing," the little Turtle said, "but I am crying." "What are you crying for?" the Coyote asked. "My mother has gone away and did not take me along," the Turtle replied, and continued to as follows:

Tingaoco, tingaoco,
Waoo, waoo, h-h-h-h (these h's spoken in quick succession while inhaling, to imitate the sobbing of a child that is sometimes heard in connection with or rather after a cry).

The Coyote again urged the Turtle to sing, as he called the crying, saying: "If you do not sing I am going to devour you." The little Turtle was very much afraid, but refused to comply with the request of the Coyote. The Coyote repeated his threat, saving, "I shall certainly devour you if you do not sing." The little Turtle, thinking of the subterfuge said: "All right, it will not hurt me; I will then simply live in your body," The Coyote said to himself, "Maybe the Turtle will continue to live in my body and move about there." And so he repeated his request, but this time changing his threat. "If you do not sing," he said, "I am going to throw you in that water there." "Don't do that, because if you do I shall drown," The Coyote did not know that the little Turtle lived in the water, and that he was being imposed upon. "All right," he said, "I shall not throw you in the water, but I shall devour you," and thereupon he took hold of the Turtle and ran towards the water. Arriving at the bank he slung the little Turtle away into the midst of the water.

"Aha! My house (Ali, Ikiningwu)," said the Turtle, and then dived into the water, but immediately came out again, saving, "Aha! My house. Thanks that you have brought me here (Ali, Ikiningwu! kwakwa, um nui pak wiki)," and, swimming around on the water, laughed at the Coyote.

The Coyote was very angry and said: "Oh! That, I did not devour you; but I am going to hunt your mother now, and if I find her somewhere, I shall certainly devour her," and thereupon ran away. Following the tracks of the Turtles, he met them on their way back to the water. They had been away quite a distance, had eaten there to their hearts' content, and were now returning. When the Coyote met them he said to the first one, "I am going to devour you," and tried to seize it. The Turtle immediately drew its head, feet and tail into the shell, and thus the Coyote, although he was working around it, throwing it over, pushing it backward and forward a long time, could not hurt it. He got very angry and jumped towards another one with the same result; so he tried others, but when he found that he could not hurt them, nor break their shell, he left them in disgust. When the Turtles arrived home, the Turtle mother gave a cactus to her child, saying: "This I brought for you," and the child ate it in great delight. "When did you awake?" the mother asked. "About half-way noon I woke up, and when I found that you were all gone I cried." "Yes," the mother said, "you were sleeping so nicely, and so I did not take you along." The little Turtle then related all about the Coyote, saying that the latter had threatened to devour it, but when he had been told that he could just do so, and that the little Turtle would then live in his body, he desisted. The Turtle mother laughed at it. The child then continued to relate how the Coyote had asked it to sing, and when refused he threatened to throw it into the water, and that he had done so, although the child had said that it would certainly drown; and the child continued, "When he threw me into the water I laughed at him and told him, 'Here I am living'; and so I got back without even getting tired."

The mother laughed at it and was very happy, saying: "Thanks that he brought you here, and that you got home even without becoming tired." And the Turtles are living there in that water still.

The Water Serpent and the Coyote

Told by Qoyawaima (Oraibi)

Listen! The people were here living (Aliksai! Yao yep yeshiwa). The Water Serpent (Balolookong) was living in Lanva, the Flute Spring, and a short distance towards the south at Ishmovala the Coyote was living. They were strong friends and often visited each other. They were still young, but the Water Serpent was already very long so that when he visited the Coyote and coiled up in his kiva he filled the entire kiva, leaving only a very small place for the Coyote, near the fireplace, where he had to sit in a crouched position. "I am going to be still larger," the Water Serpent said to him one time, "so you must enlarge your kiva." He then invited the Coyote to visit him once too, which the Coyote promised to do.

He meditated how he, too, could fill the kiva of the Water Serpent and said to the Snake: "I am going to become large and my tail will become long some day, too." While he said this the Snake was already slowly leaving the kiva, but he was so long that when the head was out already, a large part of the body was still in the kiva. After he had left, the Coyote said to himself: "Now, let me go and hunt something, too." In the evening he left the kiva and went to a place where a great deal of cedar grew. Here he pulled off a large bundle of cedar bark and carried it home. "How shall I make a tail now?" he said to himself. Soon he began to rub the cedar bark so as to make it pliable, and laying it out on the floor in a long line, wrapped it up with yucca leaves, which he had also brought with him. "But how shall I make this tail so that the Snake will not know, it?" he again asked himself, but soon formed a plan. He pulled out a lot of his hair and pasted it to the cedar bark so that it looked like a tail. This false tail he then fastened to his own tail.

In the morning when he had had his breakfast he went over to his friend, the Water Serpent. The latter had a larger kiva, so that there was sonic vacant space in it. When the Coyote had entered he kept going around the kiva dragging his long tail after him. Then he kept circling around until the kiva also was well filled, and he sat down by the head of the Water Serpent and they talked with one another. The Water Serpent smiled, thinking to himself: "Well, that tail did not used to be this way, how can that be?" After they had talked together nearly all forenoon, the Coyote said he was going home to eat his dinner, and, uncoiling his long tail, he went up the ladder, saying to the Snake: "Now, whenever you feel that way, come and visit me too again sometime," which the Snake promised to do. As the Coyote went over to his kiva dragging his long tail after him, he looked around and smilingly said to himself, "Aha, he did not find out, because he did not say anything about my tail," When he came into his kiva he went around coiling up his tail, and then untied it from his natural tail.

By and by the Snake went over to visit his friend, the Coyote, again. The latter, who had been looking for this visit, had been very much concerned about it, fearing that his friend might all at once come when he had his tail detached from his natural tail, and so was always on the lookout. Hence he saw his friend coming, and had time enough to put his tail in order again, and when the Snake arrived at the kiva he was sitting at the fireplace, ready to receive his friend. The latter began to enter, but as he had been growing considerably since his last visit, and a part of the kiva was filled with the Coyote's tail, he did not find room enough for his whole body. "I have been growing since I have been here last, and cannot get into this kiva now." "All right, let me go out," the Coyote said, "and I can talk to you from the outside while you are in the kiva. You might get cold out there." So the Coyote went out, circled around a number of times outside the kiva, coiling up his tail, and then took a seat near the kiva opening, conversing with his friend, the Water Serpent. By and by he got cold and began to wish that his friend would go home, but the latter remained. The Coyote finally got very cold and began to be secretly angry at his friend because he tarried so long. At last the latter said: "Now I must go home and eat my dinner." The Snake had not yet entirely left the kiva when the Coyote, who was very cold, rushed in and warmed himself. He was out of humor about the matter, and made up his mind to try to get even with his friend. "I am going to pay him back," he said to himself. So, after he had eaten his dinner, he thought a great deal about the matter, and in the evening went to the timber again. He brought another armful of dry cedar bark and some yucca, and made another long addition to his tail in the same manner as before, only this time he made it considerably thicker. When it was done it filled his kiva entirely. He had so well covered it with hair and wool from his body that he thought nobody would know that it was not natural.

As the Snake had invited the Coyote at his last visit to visit him. Too, sometime again, the Coyote planned to go over to his friend, but thought he would wait until there was a cold day. As in about four days it became very cold, he concluded to pay his friend a visit. Coming over to the kiva of the Snake, the two exchanged the usual greeting, the

Coyote saying, "How! (is) the friend at home?" (How! kwatch katu?) "Yes, I (am) at home. Come in." (Owe! Pai nu katu. Paki!) Whereupon the Coyote entered the kiva, and kept circling around and around, filling the entire kiva with his tail. "Well!" the Snake said, "You are going to fill this whole kiva, so let me go outside and talk to you from there." Leaving the kiva, the Water Serpent kept going around outside for some time, coiling up in such a manner that finally the head was close to the entrance so that he could talk with his friend. It was very cold and the Coyote smilingly thought to himself while he was feeling very comfortable in the warm kiva, "Now you can freeze out there, too." The Snake became very cold and wished that his friend might leave, but he tarried. The Snake was shivering and became angry and wished very much that the Coyote might take his leave. Finally the latter said that he must now go home and eat his dinner, and while the Coyote was going up the ladder dragging his tail after him, the Water Serpent went in. Arriving at the fireplace the latter said, "I am going to get even with you. I am going to pay you back;" and grabbing a stick at the fireplace, he shoved the part of the Coyote's tail that was still in the kiva on the fire, so that it caught fire, saying: "You get out of this; you (referring to the Coyote) are always taking other people's things and are always doing something bad; you had better get away from here."

The Coyote had by this time gotten away quite a distance, and, looking around, he admired his long tail. When he had nearly reached his kiva he looked around again and then noticed some smoke and fire behind him, but as there was high grass around there at that time, he thought it was the grass burning. "Oh," he said, "the Hopi have set the grass on fire. They are after me and want to drive me away. Maybe they will kill me. I am not going to my house, but I am going to run away." So he began to run westward.

Looking back he again noticed the grass burning at various places and thought he was pursued. He finally reached the timber and when he saw that burning after a while, he concluded that he would run to Little Colorado River (Bayupa) and jump in there. Then he thought the people would not find him. He did not 'yet know at this time that his tail was burning. Arriving at the river, which was very high, he jumped in and tried to swim across, but before he got across he became very tired. The river was drifting him along, and he finally sank down and drowned. The Balolookong now lived in peace at the spring forever afterwards.

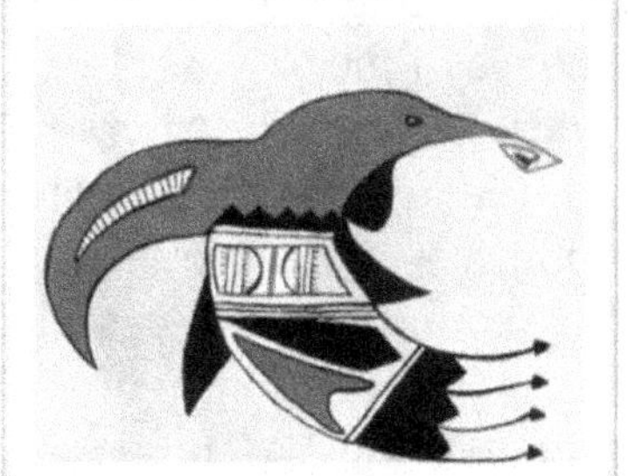

The Coyote and the Hummingbird

Told by Kwayeshva (Oraibi)

Ishyaoi! The Coyote was living at Ishmovala, west of Oraibi, and a Humming-bird was living at Tohchipchook'pu. They both had children and were good friends. One time the Coyote went to visit his friend, and as he also wanted to find some food for his children, he went north of the village to the place where the refuse of the village was thrown, and looked for some pieces of skin, old moccasins, remnants of hides, etc. The bird seeing it, went to a place close by and quickly buried itself so that the bill only was protruding. When the Coyote came to the place where the bird had buried itself, he saw something protruding from the pile of debris and said: "Thanks, I have found a needle. I shall take that home to my mother and will sew a dress for herself." So he took hold of the bill of the Humming-bird and began to pull at it. "Ishana!" the bird said, "that is my bill," and the Coyote saw that he had been fooled by his friend. The latter laughed at him.

They then went to the house of the bird, the latter entering the nest, which was built in the side of the bluff. As the Coyote could not get there, he sat on top of the bluff, and they conversed with each other. When it was nearly evening the Coyote said: "I must go home, it is evening. To-morrow you must visit me too." "All right," the Humming-bird said: "to-morrow I will come."

So they slept that night, and in the morning, after they had eaten, the bird went over to the house of the Coyote; first, however, hunting some worms in fields near by. After having eaten a number of them it went over to the Coyote's house, and saw something protruding from the ground close to the house. "Thanks, I have found a gourd jug. I am going to take this home and when my mother pops corn she will put it in here and I will eat it out of this." Hereupon she commenced pulling at the supposed jug. "Ishana!" the Coyote said, "that is my snout." Hereupon they went to the Coyote's house. That having a large entrance, the bird, of course, could go in too. The Coyote fed his friend juniper berries (lapoci), the Coyote also eating some. After they had talked a while the Humming-bird returned to her home, and the two are probably still living there.

The Coyote and the Turtle-dove

Told by Lomavantiwa (Shupaulavi)

Aliksai! The Shongopavi were living in their village, and South of the village there was a hill called Kwakchomo. There was a great deal of this grass called kwakwi there. A Turtle-dove one time was rubbing out the seed from the tassels of this grass, and while doing so cut her hand with the sharp edge of one of the blades of grass. It bled profusely, and the Turtle-dove was moaning as follows:

Hooho, hoo, hooho, hoo, hooho, hoo,
Ho-ho-ho-

While she was moaning a Coyote came along and heard somebody singing, as he believed. So he approached the place. When he arrived at the place he saw the Turtle-dove sitting and leaning forward in deep distress. "Are you singing?" he asked the Dove. "Are you thus singing?" "No," she said, "I am not singing; I am crying. I have cut myself." "No, you are singing," the Coyote replied. "Now you sing to me." "No," the Dove insisted, "I was crying," thus refusing to confirm the Coyote's statements. "Now, if you are not willing to sing to me, I shall devour you," the Coyote said. The Dove then yielded and sang the above song again. The Coyote then imitating the song of the Dove, left her and ran away.

As he was running he stumbled over a rock and fell down. As he fell he lost the song, so that he was only able to say,

"Ho-ho-ho." So the Coyote made up his mind to go back again to the Turtle-dove, and, arriving at the place where she was sitting, he began to urge her to sing. "But I am not singing," She said, "I am crying." But he would not listen, so she again sang her song to him. He again ran back, singing the Turtle-dove's song as he was running. Again he stumbled over a rock and lost the song. He again tried to sing, but could only say, "Ho-ho-ho." So he again returned to the place where the Turtle-dove had been, but the latter had gone immediately after the Coyote had left her, leaving at the place where she had been sitting a stone which very much resembled her form, and was also placed in about the position in which the Dove had been sitting. "I have fallen down again and have forgotten my song, so I came back again," the Coyote said, but he received no reply. "If you do not sing I am going to devour you," and again receiving no reply, he grabbed what he believed to be the Dove, but found that it was a stone. He broke all his teeth, and much blood was streaming from his mouth. He at once ran back and taking his way towards Shupaulavi, came to the spring Toriva, which he approached in order to drink. As he put his mouth to the water he saw a bloody face staring at him from the depth of the water. Not knowing what it was, he did not dare to drink, and ran away. Making his way northward, he ran to another spring by the name of Nankava, which is situated north of Shupaulavi. Here he again saw his reflection in the water, and did not dare to drink. He then ran to a third spring by the name of Ishk'achokpu. Seeing the same reflection in the water again, he was angry and gnarled, or rather belched, at it, from which the spring has derived its name, the Coyote Belching Water. He again was afraid to drink, but was very tired and thirsty by this time. "I am going to run to Oraibi," he said to himself; "there is a place where there is some water, and I believe there is nobody living in that place." So he ran to a place south-east of Oraibi, called

Kuritvahchikpu. When he arrived at this place he again put his snout to the water, and was just about to drink when he discovered a skeleton staring at him from the water. This time he was very angry and tore up the rocks around the spring, from which that place has derived its name. He by this time was so thirsty and exhausted that he fell down and died there.

The Coyote and the Blue Jays

Told by Wikvaya (Oraibi)

Haliksai! A long time ago the people lived in Oraibi. West of the village, at Ishmovala, lived the Coyote and his wife. They had six children and the Coyote used to go and hunt rabbits for his children. One day he went hunting again and found a little cottontail rabbit, which he chased. The rabbit ran into the hole, which the Coyote could not enter. "How shall I get this rabbit out now?" he thought to himself; then somebody came along; it was the Badger. "You get this out for me here," the Coyote said, "I want this rabbit for my children to eat." So the Coyote sat down and waited while the Badger scratched a hole until he reached the rabbit, whereupon he pulled the latter out. The Coyote was very happy. "Thus," he said, "on your account my children will have something to eat." Then the Coyote took the rabbit in his mouth and ran home with it, being very happy. When he arrived in his home the little Coyotes wrangled over the rabbit, tore it to pieces and devoured it, some of them getting something, others not, so they remained hungry.

The next morning both the Coyote and his wife went out in search of food again, the latter ascending up to the village, and ran past the village on the west side, then by the north side, turning northward over the mesas. Not finding anything, she finally entered the woods north of the village.

All at once she heard something in the trees, and, looking up, she saw some Blue Jays in the tree. The Blue jays were dancing in the tree and she coveted them. They said to the Coyote: "We are having a dance here, you come and be with us and assist us." "I would like to," the Coyote said, "but how shall I get up there?" "Why, we shall lend you some of our wings, tails, and feathers," the Blue jays said. "All right," she said. So they took off some of their wings, tails, and feathers and put them on her legs. They then told her that she must dance and sing just the same as they did, and then they again began to sing.

The Coyote now having wings ascended and danced with them. When they had finished the song they all flew away, the Coyote with them, and alighted on some other tree. This they repeated in all three times. They then flew up high into the air, the Coyote with them, and when they were very high up they all surrounded the Coyote, each one saying: "This is my tail, this is my wing, these are my feathers," and then tore out all the feathers that they had loaned the Coyote. When they had torn out all the feathers the Coyote began to fall downward to the earth. When she reached it she was dead.

Her children still had nothing to eat. When the Coyote father saw that his wife was not coming home he concluded that he would go and hunt her. Following her tracks, he ascended to the village, passed the village on the west side, and when he reached the north side of the village the dogs of the village noticed him and pursued him. He at once left the footprints of his wife and ran back to his children. So after that the little Coyotes had no mother. The Coyote then afterwards hunted food alone for his children, and that is the reason why so many Coyotes have to look out for their food alone.

The Coyote and the Eagle

Aliksai! North of Shupaulavi is the Katcina House (Katcinki). West of this is a bluff, and on top of this bluff used to live an Eagle. One time the Coyote came along. "What are you wandering around for?" the Eagle asked. "Yes," the Coyote said. The Eagle was standing on one foot, having the other foot hidden in his feathers. The Coyote was wondering, and asked: "Why are you standing on one foot?" "Yes," the Eagle said, "I cut one leg off, and so I am standing on one foot." "Is that so?" the Coyote said, and was thinking. "I am envious at you," he said to the Eagle; "I shall try to stand on one leg too; but how did you cut your leg off, bow is that done?" "Why," the Eagle replied, "you just lay your leg across a stone and strike on it with a sharp stone and then it will be cut off, it does not hurt, and you need not be afraid."

So the Coyote hunted for a sharp stone and there was another sharp stone with a sharp edge. He laid his right hind leg across the latter, raised the small sharp stone and cut off his leg. Hereupon the Eagle lowered his second leg, stretched out his wings, and laughed at the Coyote and said: "I have two legs, see here." "Oh!" the Coyote said, "I, poor one, that I thoughtlessly cut off my leg." And while the Eagle flew away the Coyote was crying, and, limping away, probably perished somewhere.

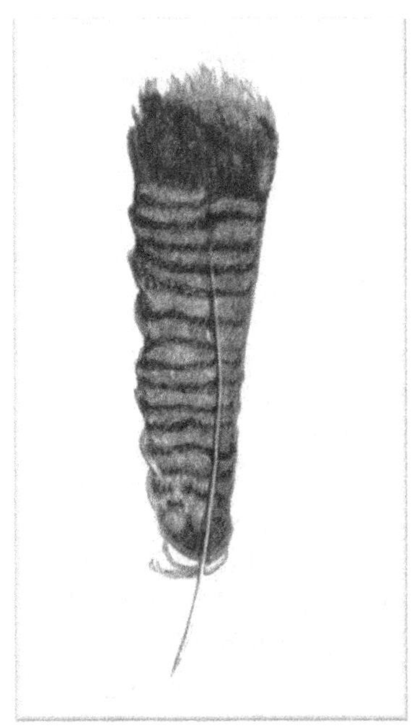

The Coyote and the Turkeys

Told by Kwayeshva (Oraibi)

Haliksai! At Ishmovala the Coyote was living, and at Nuvatuk'aovi, a short distance east of Ishmovala, the Turkey lived. They both had children and were great friends, and often visited each other. One time when the Coyote came to the house of the Turkeys they fed him pinon nuts, which he relished very much. The little Turkeys were very nicely figured, and the Coyote enjoyed looking at them. He envied them for their beautiful feathers and was wondering how they were figured so nicely. As he looked at them he stroked their bodies with a forepaw. "Yes," the Turkey mother said, "I baked these, my children. I put them into an oven and baked them, then I ate their meat, but I did not break any bones, nor did I bite into any bones. Them I left entirely unhurt. Early in the morning I put them into a tray, waved them up and down, singing the following song over them:

Pipichacha, pipichacha (archaic).
Talahoya, huwamu, itimu!
Wake up, please, my children!

Then I threw all the bones outside and there my children got alive again, and since then they are so beautifully figured." She was, of course, deceiving him. "Oh!" the Coyote said; "yes, these are very pretty, and I shall do the same."

In the evening he returned to his house and early the next morning he went after wood. Returning with the wood, he heated his oven. He made the oven very hot, then took one of his children and pitied it, but the little Turkeys had been so pretty and he had so envied them for their pretty figuring, that he threw the little Coyote into the oven. Hereupon another one, and another one, as he had a great many children. He threw them into the oven until the oven was full. He placed a stone over the opening and plastered up the oven. While they were being baked in the oven he ground some corn to make some hurushiki. So in the evening he took them out of the oven and found them thoroughly baked. He took out one after another and then commenced to eat. They tasted very fine. He ate all the meat, but the bones he did not hurt. He did not break any, nor did he crush any with his teeth. Gathering the bones into a basket he went to sleep.

During the night the Turkey mother said to her children: "We had better flee away from here on account of your uncle, the Coyote, because he will be very angry and will certainly come and devour us." Hereupon she sent her children away to the San Francisco Mountains (near Flagstaff). She took the pelts, blankets, etc., in which they had been sleeping, and rolling some of the smaller ones up, placed them on the floor and covered them up so as to make them appear as if they were still sleeping, under the covering. Hereupon she followed her children.

The Coyote in the meanwhile got up once and looked whether the sun was not yet rising, but it was still dark. After a while he looked again and then the sun came out.

He at once took the tray (tuchaiya) containing the bones of his children, went out with it, waved it up and down the way the Turkey Woman had shown him, and sang the song which she had told him she had sung over the bones of her children. Hereupon he also threw the bones away. But alas! nothing became alive, and only the bones were lying there. When he saw what had happened he cried bitterly and became very angry. "I shall go over to the house of the Turkey," he said, "and shall certainly devour the little Turkeys too." Hereupon he went over to his friend's house, running very fast. When he came to the house he at once entered and thought they were all sleeping nicely. He jumped upon their beds and grabbed what he believed to be the young Turkeys, but found that nobody was there. They had deceived him. "Ah," he said, "they have run away, but I shall certainly overtake them." So he rushed out, hunted up the tracks of the Turkeys and followed them running very fast. While the Coyote was following their tracks, the Turkeys had arrived at the Little Colorado River, but when they had crossed it the little Turkeys were very tired. "I shall leave you here," their mother said, "and run ahead of you." But one of the little ones was crying very bitterly. The Turkey mother ran ahead to the San Francisco Mountains and informed the Turkeys living there about what had happened. "You that are strong come quickly and help us; the Coyote is following us and he will kill my children. You go quickly and get them." So two of the Turkey men that were very strong came out and ran towards the place where the Turkey mother had left her children. The latter, however, remained because she was very tired.

The Coyote in the meanwhile found the little Turkeys and chasing them, said: "Aha, I shall devour you" (Ali kurzh nu umui cowani). The little Turkeys were running around and crying very bitterly. just as the Coyote was about to take one of the little Turkeys the two Turkey men came upon him, grabbed the little ones, of which there were two, took them on their backs and ran away with them. "Why do you take them away?" the Coyote cried. "I am hungry and I want to eat them. That is the reason why I followed them." But they did not listen, and as they were strong and the Coyote was very tired, he had to return to his home hungry. But before he got home he died.

The Chiro and the Coyote

Told by Qoyawaima (Oraibi)

In Oraibi the people were living. At Ishmovala the Coyote lived. Away over there at K'ahk'angwovakaavi lived a great many Chiros, and they were always dancing there. One time the Coyote was walking about east of their village. The Chiros saw him as they were dancing. They were singing as follows:

Ishawu, ishawu, hohoongyanikay colmoki
Coyote, Coyote, to dance is longing,
Ishawu, oomii hongina,
Coyote upward dances,
Aatk'amii hongina,
Downward dances,
Machiwa, machiwa, chirororoi.
Is called, is called chirororoi.

The Coyote was looking at them and wanted to dance along. "Very well," the Chiros said to him, whereupon each one of them gave him some feathers; one some wing feathers, another some tail feathers, and so on. They made for the Coyote wings and a tail, and put small feathers into his body, whereupon the Coyote was very happy. "Thanks," he said, "that you have made wings for me. I am going to dance with you now." Hereupon they danced, again singing the same song. The Coyote danced with them. Now they were flying upward somewhere, and arrived somewhere away high up. Now they crowded around the Coyote and said: "Why, this is my wing; why, this is my tail; why, these are my feathers;" some of them had given him these things, and now they took everything away from him, and alas! he began to descend. He arrived at the earth and died. The Chiros laughed at him. "Thanks," they said, "that you have died, because you very often do commit depredations on some one's property. That is why you were going about again."

The Coyote and the Porcupine

Told by Sik'ahpik'i (Shupaulavi)

At some distance southwest of Walpi is a place called Water Killing Hill (Baqoychomo), where there are still some old ruins. A short distance north of this place is a place called Skeleton Hill (Maschomo). At these two places the people from Oraibi, Walpi, and the other villages rested with their captives after they had destroyed Aoatovi, taking with them many men, women, and children. Here at these places, it is said, they extorted from their captives the secrets of their ceremonies and altars, and after they had learned everything from them, they killed a good many of them, probably torturing some of them. Tradition says that in some cases they cut women's breasts off and left them to perish. From this killing of those captives these two places have derived their names.

At the first named place the Porcupine used to live, a long time ago, while the Coyote was living at the last named place. One time the Coyote went to visit his friend, the

Porcupine. "Sit down," the latter said. "All right," the Coyote said, and so they talked together a long time. When it was noon the Porcupine said: "We are going to eat something. You build a fire;" so the Coyote built a large fire. When the Coyote had built the fire the Porcupine said: "Now we are going to have something to eat." So he drew a small pointed stick from his hair on the top of his head and thrust it into his nose. After he had done this repeatedly, blood and fat dropped out of his nose on the fire, where it was roasted. This he handed to the Coyote to eat. So they were eating. "Aha," the Porcupine said: "thus I am preparing food." "Yes," the Coyote said, "we are happy."

So after they had eaten they conversed until evening; then the Coyote said, "I must go home now." "Very well," the Porcupine replied, "it is evening now," "But you must visit me too, to-morrow," the Coyote said, and thereupon left, the Porcupine saying laughingly, "You will have something good too, since you have seen it here." So the next morning the Porcupine went over to his friend and there sure enough found that the Coyote also had a pointed stick thrust into his hair. When it was noon again the Porcupine also built a fire at his friend's kiva. "We are going to eat something fine," the Coyote said. So the Coyote pulled out his stick, drew close up to the fire, bent over it, and also began to poke his nose with the stick, whereupon also blood, mixed with fat or tallow, began to come out. It covered the fire, and finally began to flow away, and wouldn't stop. The Coyote's nose was bleeding and bleeding, and finally he became exhausted and fell down.

The Porcupine, thinking that his friend had died, laughed, and without having eaten anything, left the kiva and went home. He was angry at his friend because he wanted to imitate him, and now was not successful. By and by the Coyote revived. The blood had stopped flowing, forming large hard pieces of coagulated blood and grease in front of his nose. He was very angry. "That friend of mine," he said, "that friend is the cause that this happened to me; he wanted it this way. I am going to devour him." So after he had become strong again the next morning, he went over to his friend to attack him. When he arrived there he looked down, and his friend looking up noticed the blood on his nose. "Well now, have you not died? I thought you had died, and that is the reason why I went away." "Yes," the Coyote said very roughly, "you have bewitched me. On your account I almost died, and now I have come over here to devour you." "No, no," the Porcupine said, "you are not going to devour me. Why, you are my friend, and a friend will not eat up his friend. No, indeed." Then he began to talk kindly to his friend saying: "Well, since you have not died, we will live together again." The Coyote then also quieted down and they conversed together amicably. They then lived there again as friends, the Coyote thinking that he would have a chance sometime to take revenge on the Porcupine.

The Coyote and the Badger

Told by Kiwanhongva (Oraibi)

Haliksai! In the village they were living, and south of La'nangva at Coyote Gap (Ishmovala) the Coyote was living. At Badger Gulch (Honancika), about one-eighth of a mile south-east of Oraibi, lived the Badger. These two were great friends with each other, and often visited each other. One time the Oraibi were cleaning out the spring of La'nangva, in which the maidens of the village assisted. They had taken their food along, which they placed near a rock not far from the spring. Towards evening the chief said: "Now get your food and let us eat." So they spread blankets on the ground and placed the food on it and ate. After they were through they went to the village.

The Coyote was sitting a short distance away watching the people as they ate, and envied them. Early the next morning he heard the crier announce another spring cleaning. As soon as the Coyote heard this announcement he ran over to his friend, the Badger. Arriving at the latter's house, he asked: "Is my friend in?" "Yes," the latter replied, "come in!" "Very well," the Coyote said, "but I am in a hurry. These Oraibi are going to clean the spring again and they have something very fine to eat there. Let us go over and take part in the eating, but do not be slow. Follow me soon." "Very well," the Badger said. Hereupon the Coyote left, the Badger soon following him. They entered the

Coyote's house, and from there the Badger commenced to dig a hole towards the place where the food was, and after he had gone a little way he turned around, which is the custom, of the badgers. The Coyote noticed it and said: "Oh! you are turning back again." "Yes," the Badger replied, "that is the way I dig. We must not be alone in this." "Yes," the Coyote said, here is some one else close by. He digs straight ahead."

Hereupon the Coyote left his house and ran over to a place a short distance east of his house where the Mole (Mu'yi) lived. He entered the latter's house and said: "The people are cleaning the spring there and they have a great deal of food there, of which we want to get some. But the Badger, who has been digging towards it, always turns around, and we shall not get there. You come and scratch a hole for us and we shall give you a great deal of it." The Mole was at once willing and said: "Very well, I shall come," and went along with the Coyote. After entering the Coyote's house the Mole at once commenced to dig a hole underground, which he did very rapidly. The Badger followed him, enlarging the hole. The Coyote followed the Badger and scratched out the loose dirt.

They arrived at a place not far from the rock where the food had been placed the day before. Here the Mole made a small opening and looked out and saw that the people were just arriving, and that the maidens again placed the food near the rock. So the Mole continued his digging to the place where the food was, and while the Hopi were at work, he reached all the food to his companions. The Mole handed it to the Badger, the Badger to the Coyote, and the latter carried it to his house. When the Hopi were through with their work the chief again said to the maidens that they should now go and get their food. They would eat and then go home. So the maidens raced towards the rock where they had placed the food, but when they arrived here they found all their food gone. They looked around and found a hole in the ground, but only for a short distance, because the Badger had tightly closed up the hole from the inside. "Well now," the maidens said, "somebody has put our food in here." So the men and the youths brought their hoes and followed the opening in the ground, but they soon found that it was only open a short distance. Hereupon they abandoned it and went home hungry.

In the Coyote's house the three now divided up the food and the Badger and the Mole carried home their portions. On this they lived for some time afterwards. Soon afterwards the Coyote again visited the Badger. The Badger had cut up into small pieces some lolo'okongs and roasted them. They were very fat. This food he set before his friend, the Coyote, and with it some comiviki. The Coyote ate the food with relish. "But that tastes well," he said; "what is it? Where did you get it?" "Why, I opened my side," the Honani said. "My intestines are covered with much fat, and I took out some of that fat and prepared this food from it," "Did it not hurt you," the Coyote asked, "when you opened your body?" "No," the Badger replied, "I opened it, took out the fat, and you see there is nothing the matter with my body. With this knife here I opened my body," showing the knife to the Coyote. "Very well," the Coyote said, "I am going to take this knife along and I am going to do the same, so to-morrow you must visit me, too." Hereupon he left and went home.

The Badger laughed, saying: "That Fool Old Man (Una Wuhtaka) believes that I took that fat out of my body."

The next morning the Coyote took the knife and commenced to cut into his abdomen. It hurt him very much, 'and as he was cutting he moaned, "Ana-na-na," but he kept on cutting and the blood was running out profusely. When he had cut through the abdomen wall he took hold of the fat and commenced to pull at it, but before he got through he became exhausted and fell down and died. When his friend, the Badger, arrived he found the Coyote lying there dead. "That Fool Old Man," he said, "thinking that I extracted that fat from my body!" And thus the Badger killed his friend, the Coyote.

The Squirrel and the Chipmunk

Told by Qowawaima (Oraibi)

A long time ago the Squirrel and the Chipmunk lived near the Nose Gulch (Pongoyakvoco), the Squirrel living on the north side and the Chipmunk on the south side. The two were good friends and often visited each other. Near by were some peach orchards, where a certain old man owned a number of trees, There the two would go every day and eat peaches. The Chipmunk relished the peaches, while the Squirrel preferred the kernels from the stone. The Chipmunk would climb the trees, break open the peaches, and eating the flesh of the peaches, throw down the seeds to the Squirrel; or the Chipmunk would also throw down peaches, which the Squirrel would put in its mouth and carry to a certain place on the rock, where the two afterwards would feast on them.

They were careful that the owner of the peach orchard would not find them there, because they knew that the latter made very desperate efforts, to capture and kill them. One time the Squirrel said to the Chipmunk: "We ought to have a little dance some time. When you go ho-.me you try to make a song and then come and sing it to me. And then when we go to eat peaches again we shall have a little dance there and sing the little song." So the Chipmunk went home and thought over the matter and tried very hard to compose a song. Finally he concluded to make a song about his friend, the Squirrel, and when he was done he went over and sang it to the Squirrel. The latter at first was not very much pleased and said: "Why you have song-tied me, you have made a song about me." "Yes," the Chipmunk said, "I did not know what to sing, and as we always go and eat peaches together and have such a good time there and then lie down on the rock together, I thought I would compose a song about that." This satisfied the Squirrel. They then practiced the song together, which was as follows:

Lakana, lakana!
Squirrel, squirrel!
Oyu nalaa,
Satisfied alone.
Oatu owaka
(The) rock on top
Pushickatcii--
Lying stretched out;
Hinahina, hinahina.

You have spoken correctly, the Squirrel said, "We are living in plenty." Hereupon they went to the peach orchard again to eat peaches but found the old man in the orchard, so they waited a little while until he had done his work and had gone to sleep under one of the trees. They then carried a great many peaches as usual, to the place on the rock where they generally feasted, and after they had filled themselves they had a little dance, singing their song. They stood on their hind legs holding their front paws upward. The old man awoke from the noise of the singing, and when he saw, them he at once knew that they were the culprits who destroyed and carried away his peaches, so he ran towards them, saying: "Aha, why are you making noise? I have found you. You are naughty, and I am going to kill you," and saying this he tried to climb the rock upon which they were. They jumped down, however, and both rushed into the house of the Squirrel at the foot of the rock. The old man followed them and when he saw where they had gone, he waited. The two were very happy and laughed at their pursuer. The Chipmunk looked up and said: "Aha, there he is watching us. I am going to get out, pass him, and run to my house. He cannot catch me." "All right," the Squirrel said, "try it." So the Chipmunk, rushed out. The man ran after it furiously, trying to kill it, and had almost overtaken it when the Chipmunk had reached its house and rushed into it,

After that the two did not fear the old man and continued to live off his peach orchard, being careful, however, that he did not catch them. And so ever since the Squirrel and Chipmunk are not very much afraid of the Hopi and destroy and eat their peaches. Had the old man at that time killed the two, such would not be the case now.

A Bet between the Cooyoko and the Fox

Told by Sik'aletsiwa (Shupaulavi)

Aliksai! In Shupaulavi, north of the village, is a bluff where there is a place called Cooyoko House (Cooyok-ki). Here the Cooyoko lived. One time a Fox, who was very handsome, came along, and the Cooyoko Uncle (Tahaam) was sitting on the edge of the bluff when the Fox came along. The sun had not yet risen, and the Cooyoko was sitting and waiting to watch the sunrise. "Come here," he said to the Fox, "come to me here." "All right," the Fox said and came. "Sit down, sit down with me," the Cooyoko said, which the Fox did. "Now," the Cooyoko continued, "let us have a contest and see upon whose song the sun will rise. The one that loses shall be killed with this knife here," which the Cooyoko had, the Fox said. "Yes," the Cooyoko said, "let us have a contest." "All right," the Fox said, "be it so. You sing first." So the Cooyoko sang the following little song:

To -- ishkakolitai to -- ishkakolitai
Aaha, iiihi--

And then said to the Fox: "Now, you sing, too," whereupon the Fox sang the following song:

Ishka! Ishka!

Hereupon the Cooyoko repeated his song. The sun by this time was just about to loom up. "Now you sing again," he said to the Fox, whereupon the latter repeated his song, and when he was singing, the sun loomed upon the horizon. So he had won the contest. "Alas!" the Cooyoko said, "well now, I have wanted it this way and you have beaten me. Be it so then." The knife was lying by their side, so the Fox took it, approached the Cooyoko, and cut the latter's throat. And so the latter died over a bet.

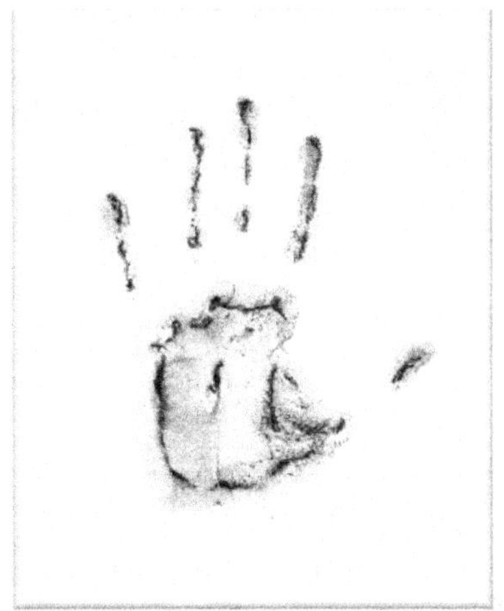

The Little Gray Mice and the Little Brown Mice

Told by Qoyawaima (Oraibi)

A long time ago the Little Gray Mice (Povo'yamu) lived at Tumble Down Bluff (Tukwishahpukpu), south-east of the village, and the Little Brown Mice (Pavavumshamu) lived at Chirove, west of the village, far down the mesa. The two kinds of mice were on friendly terms at that time. During the night they would come to the village and whenever one would find hidden away in jars or packed away in the rooms, corn, etc., it would invite the others and then they would come and carry away the food to their holes. This they did a long time. The two kinds of mice would often visit each other and dance together. They would usually sing the following song, both parties it seems generally using the same words:

Talawyayna talawyaynaaa
It begins to dawn, it begins to dawn.
Ahaha, ihihi. Talawyayna, talawyaynana,
Yaoohoo, oohia, ahaha ihihi.

One time one of the Gray Mice had found something very good to eat, perhaps peaches, and ran over to the Brown Mice, saving: "I have found some good food and I have already made a hole in the cover so that we can get at it." Hereupon they all came from both places, but when they were carrying their food away to their houses they commenced to quarrel over it and had a great fight. Many were bitten, although none were killed. After a few days the Gray Mice went over to the Brown Mice again, entered their kiva and danced. They changed their song somewhat, however, singing as follows:

Talawyayna, talawyayna.
It begins to dawn, it begins to dawn.
Ahaha ihihi,
Talawyayna, talawyayna, ahaha, ihihi,
Yaoohoo oohio,
Pas nu pawupshat wupashurut
Very I (of) big mice, long tails
Mamkashi, (afraid), Pi nuu, pi nuu! O! I! O! I!
Yaoohoo oohia
Pas nu yan toonumkat mamkashi
Very I thus whistlers afraid (of)
Pi! nuu! pi, nuu! Pu yaami! Pu yaami.
O! I! O! I! Now off! now off!

When they were through singing they rushed out of the kiva back to their home. The Brown Mice laughed at them, saying: "Aha, they are afraid of us." The two kinds of mice have never been on good terms since, and from that time they began to scatter out through the fields and through the houses, and that is the reason why they now may be found everywhere.

The Badger and the Small Grey Mice

Told by Qoyawaima (Oraibi)

A long time ago a Badger lived north of the village of Oraibi. He was a doctor and the people used to go to him seeking aid and cure for their various ailments. The place where he lived was called Badger Burrow (Honan Yaha); the Small Gray Mice (Tucanhomihtci) or rather many of them, lived west of Oraibi at a place called Big Hill (Wopachmo).

One time the Hopi were on a hunt west of this place, where those Mice lived, and as ill luck would have it, one of the hunters hit another one with his boomerang and broke his leg. Nobody seemed to take interest enough in the unfortunate man to care for him, so he tried to get home the best he could. Seeing a light at the aforesaid Big Hill, he made for that place and found an underground room similar to the Hopi kivas. In it he observed a number of small people like children. They at once noticed him, saying: "Somebody is looking in here," and invited him to come down. "How can I come in?" he said. "What is the matter with you?" they asked, to which he replied: "My thigh bone is broken." So one of the small men went up the ladder and carried the lame man down, placing him on the floor north of the fireplace. Two rabbits, which the man had killed and brought with him from the hunt, he left outside. The people pitied the poor man and said: "So this has happened to you." "Yes," he answered, "could not one of you hunt me up a doctor?" Whereupon one of the small men whispered to another one: "Let's repair the leg for him." "All right," he answered, who was a chief. Hereupon a door was opened on the north side of the kiva which led into another room, and all the small people, who seemed to be children, were sent into that small room. One of the men, who took care of the fire at the fireplace, remained with the sick man. The one who remained, presently called out: "Now come in here," whereupon a very great number of the Mice entered the room, crowded around the patient, covering him completely, and commencing to rub him all over the body and otherwise worked on and about him, and in that way plied their art as doctors upon the patient that had so unexpectedly dropped in upon them. All at once they all ran away, entered another room again, and the man found that his leg had been made well. He was very happy and leaving the two rabbits as a remuneration, he went home to the village. The people knowing that his leg had been broken the previous day, were surprised to see him well and inquired who had cured him. He told them.

The Badger, who lived north of the village, heard about it and became very jealous and angry about the matter. The man whose leg had been healed by the Mice said to the people, that the "Old Man Badger" was somewhat behind. It had been those Mice who had cured him and what was more, they had not asked for any pay, whereas, the Old Man Badger always asked something for his services, meat, cactus bulbs, etc., and he advised people who ever had any ailments, to go to these Mice physicians that lived west of the village, and had cured him. The Old Man Badger did a great deal of thinking over the matter and was angry. Finally he concluded that he was going to test the knowledge of the Mice doctors. "I am going to feign sickness and shall call them over, and if they can tell me my ailment, I shall believe in them." So he feigned sickness; placed some pelts and blankets on the floor and a bowl by his side, and laid down. In order to make it appear that he was very sick he took a little nourishment in the morning only and kept expectorating into the bowl. This he did for three days, at the end of which he looked very tired and exhausted. So he called some one who was passing by and said to him: "You go over there to those Mice doctors and fetch them here, because I am very sick." So this man went over and told them that that poor Old Man Badger was very sick and seemed to be dying, and that they should have pity on him and come over there the next day. Having delivered this message to them, he returned to his home. They were willing, and their chief taking the lead, they went to the mesa, passed by the village on the north side, along the edge of the mesa, to the dwelling of the Badger. This dwelling consisted of a kiva like the Hopi kivas of to-day. The Badger was still angry and had hidden a stick under his bed. The mice, however, had brought no medicines with them. Arriving at the kiva, the chief went down the ladder first, passing by the east side of the fireplace to the bed of the patient. He was followed by his companions, of whom there were many, who also crowded around the bed of the sick doctor. The latter was groaning very much, acting as if he was about to die. The chief of the Mice doctors then began to sing the following song in which he was accompanied by all the others:

Cowiskwi naiukwiwiwaa!
Rabbit meat cook for us!

To which the Badger replied in a faint voice:

Ham pai pi pam himuu shulawu.
Oh why this something all gone.

The Mice kept slowly moving on in a circle and soon commenced to sing

Aahai! aahai! Ayam hapiii,
Honanyahay epee
At the Badger burrow over there.
Honanwuhatka
The Badger Old Man
Tucun Homihtcit
The Tucan Homcihtci
Aotuhik unangwyat
A doctor to be believed
Aonawotcniekae
Because he heard
Naloshwat aknachangkwainitaa Hahahaha
Four times he fasted
Hainawa Hainawa (No meaning.)
Hainawa Hainawa

Free rendering:

At the Badger burrow the Badger
Old man heard that the Tusan
Homihtsi believed himself to be a
Doctor and hence fasted four days.

The Mouse doctor sang this in order to let the Badger know that he had at once detected the fraud. Being through with the singing, he told the Badger that nothing was the matter with him; as soon as he would eat something he would get well.

While they were singing they had kept slowly going around the bed of the sick doctor and when they were through with their singing they had reached the ladder. The leader, after having given the Badger his opinion as mentioned above, at once ascended the ladder, being followed by all the others. The Badger was very angry by this time, and grabbing the stick which he had hidden under his bed, he began to strike at some of the Mice, but as he had fasted so long, and the Mice jumped around in the kiva and up the ladder very fast, he failed to hit any of them. he tried to follow them, but failed to catch and kill any of them for the same reason. But some of the younger Mice could not keep up with the older ones while they were running to their home, being chased by the Badger, so they scattered out, and not being able to find their way home, they dug holes for themselves, and that is the reason why these mice, "Homihtsi," are now living all over the country. The Badger is the cause of this scattering of these Mice.

But these new settlers had nothing to eat, so they went to hunt food, and wherever they came upon some seed or plant they would appropriate them, and to this day, wherever the Hopi plant something, these Mice will come and eat it. If that Old Man Badger had not scattered them at that time they would not be all over the country now, but would still be living at the one place west of the village, where they had their home at that time. But, on the other hand, if any Hopi works in his field or travels anywhere, or is away from his village for any purpose, and if he becomes sick, or gets hurt, these Mice in all unseen secret way take care of him so that he does not die; but they do not come to the village to take care of any sick.

www.ingramcontent.com/pod-product-compliance
Lightning Source LLC
Chambersburg PA
CBHW070352200726
48294CB00003B/859

* 9 7 8 1 7 3 7 7 1 0 0 2 8 *